Introduction to Public Policy

Second Edition

Introduction to Public Policy

Second Edition

Jong Youl Lee
&
Chad Anderson

Daeyoung Moonhwasa Publishing Company
Seoul, Republic of Korea

Introduction to Public Policy
Second Edition

Jong Youl Lee
(Professor, Incheon National University)

Chad Anderson
(Assistant Professor, Incheon National University)

Ilustration Jeoung Jae Hong

ISBN 978-89-7644-537-7
Published by Lim Choon Whan
Daeyoung Moonhwasa Publishing Co.
5, Cheongpa-ro 61-gil, Yongsan-gu, Seoul, 04308, Korea

TEL (02) 716-3883, (02) 714-3062
FAX (02) 703-3839
First edition published on 5 March, 2008
Second edition published on 5 January, 2016

Price ₩13,000

Preface

The first edition of the book was published seven years ago but the need for it has, if anything, grown during those years. Apart from steady demand for it in Korean college classrooms, the Korean youth job market remains unattractive enough that the Korean Labor Foundation reports 35% of non-employed young college graduates are studying for civil service exams or otherwise preparing for public employment. Therefore there is great and increasing demand for an understanding of the policy process for employment. At the same time, the passage of time has called for updated references and more recent examples more familiar to current readers. All weaknesses revealed by the years of heavy use are also corrected here.

If you are reading this book, you probably want to work in some form of public service and are hopefully politically active and vote. You can benefit from understanding the public policy process. It is a process of making decisions that has much to teach people to help them in their individual lives. In addition, the overall process is basically the same no matter what sort of government and polity rule in your jurisdiction, whether you are from Korea or some other country. This is because the public policy process is a technical process that is compatible with any national value system.

The public policy process requires clarification of values. This is done through political processes where different public actors weigh in and contribute to a collective definition and sense of meaning. While values need to be clear, they may be clear implicitly through the nature of the system, rather than explicitly through formal statements. There is no requirement for what the values must be. The process applies in any country.

The policy process is a systematic process for making quality decisions within a given values framework. The emphasis of the process is on making decisions of the highest quality with the most efficient use of resources in a particular policy-making framework.

Residents and citizens are part of this system, consume media, and participate in the political process. When you do not participate, you assert that your values are not important and hand over the process to others and let them make the decisions that affect your life. An understanding of public policy can help you evaluate the information you take in, clarify public debates, and make informed citizen decisions that are consistent with your individual values.

This process is analogous to the decision-making process you use in your private life. Your decisions at work and at home are not always consistent and so do not reinforce each other. Everyone can benefit from a systematic approach to decisions. The successful student of public policy will start to improve their personal life as a systematic approach to problem-solving takes the place of the haphazard approach that results from a lack of consideration.

This course can help you live a better life, be a better and more effective citizen, and prepare for the real world of work, whether in the corporate or public sector. Take it seriously and the benefits will be significant.

Finally, no book belongs to the authors alone. A listing of the many people who provided us support and advice would be a listing of the many friends and family members who encouraged us. However, our publisher Lim Choon Whan deserves special mention for supporting and advancing our work in spite of difficulties in the publishing business. In addition, Dr. Jiyoung Ro and Dr. M. Sohel Iqbal made a critical contribution to the first edition that forms the basis for this book. To them and to all who have offered assistance and advice, we owe a deep gratitude.

Jong Youl Lee

Chad Anderson

Incheon, December 2015

Contents

List of Figures

List of Tables

WEEK 1 Introduction

Summary

Public policy consists of actions made in the public's name, made by government or at least initiated by government. Public policy is interpreted and implemented by public and private actors.

It includes both what government intends to do and what government chooses not to do. It is defined as in the public interest, but there is debate over what constitutes the true public interest. Public policy is studied for scientific purposes of learning truth or for more practical professional and political reasons.

1 What is Public Policy?

Public policy is normally thought of as government action to address a problem or problems. The central focus is who gets what when and how. Policies are revealed through texts, practices, symbols, and discourses that define and deliver values through goods and services as well as regulations, income, status, and other positively or negatively valued attributes. Public policy is basically government action or inaction taken in response to social problems.

Social problems are conditions the public widely perceives to be unacceptable that require intervention. Personal or private problems like bad grades or low sales are not the same as social problems such as environmental degradation, workplace safety, or access to health care that can be addressed through government action, private action (meaning that individuals or private organizations like businesses and NGOs take the responsibility), or a combination of the two. Any level of government (central, urban, provincial, local) may be involved in a policy effort. This is because social problems, and the public demand for action to address them, manifest themselves from the local to the national level, or even internationally. At the local level there are problems like traffic congestion. At the national level there are issues like power generation and the response to climate change.

[Figure 1-1] Traffic Congestion : A Local Problem

Defining Public Policy

Birkland speaks to the difficulty of defining public policy, noting that there are many different definitions that vary depending on the perspective of the user (Birkland, 2001). Therefore, Table 1-1 presents several such definitions. However, public policy can be defined by five traits (Birkland, 2001):

- Policy made in the "public's" name
- Policy generally made or initiated by government
- Policy interpreted and implemented by public and private actors
- Something government intends to do
- Something government chooses not to do

Sabatier speaks to the complexity of defining public policy as part of the policy process:

"In short, understanding of the policy process requires knowledge of the goals and perceptions of hundreds of actors throughout the country involving possibly very technical scientific and legal issues over periods of a decade or more while most of those actors are actively seeking to propagate their specific spin on events" (Sabatier, 2007: 4).

Therefore, there are a broad variety of potential definitions that depend on the technical, scientific, legal, political, and institutional orientation of the actors in the process advancing the definitions. At any rate, public policy is related to government and public institutions or organizations recognized as acting on behalf of the public interest. It is related to formal and informal rules and laws and implicit and explicit intents.

[Table 1-1] Defining Public Policy

Definition	Author
"Whatever governments choose to do or not to do."	Dye (1992)
"Public policy is the outcome of the struggle in government over who gets what."	Cochran et al. (1999)
"In studying policy, then, we look at the broader sweep of politics, not simply the written laws and rules themselves."	Birkland (2001)
"The combination of basic decisions, commitments, and actions made by those who hold or influence government positions of authority."	Gerston (2010)
"Public policy is defined here as what government ought or ought not do, and does or does not do."	Simon (2009)

2 Why Public Policy?

The dominant ideological foundation of modern constitutional systems following the American Constitution is known as classical liberalism. Among the many beliefs stemming from liberalism is the belief that power is derived from the consent of the governed. This means that "the people" are the governed, but they also provide their consent to the government. As a result, when policy advocates seek to induce the government to make policy (by taking an action or refusing to do so), proponents of the new policy will claim that the government does so in the "public interest."

However, controversies arise because there is disagreement over what constitutes "the public interest." For example, those who argue that Korea needs more government workers to match the average size of OECD governments claim to do so to bring the proper level of public services to Korean citizens. On the other hand, when Seoul announced its plans to lay off 1300 government workers, former Mayor Oh Sehoon claimed the decision was about ending waste and providing efficient government, another definition of the public interest. Some policy advocates claim that laws that relieve tax burdens on the rich are in the public interest because they create overall public wealth. On the other hand those who argue that the rich should be taxed at a higher rate than the poor claim that taxation based on ability to pay is more in the spirit of the public interest.

Another example of disputes over what policies should be made in the broader public interest is the issue of the minimum wage. Recent controversies regarding the minimum wage have emerged in Korea regarding publicizing, enforcing, and raising the minimum wage, including a petition campaign for a 10,000₩ minimum wage. Each side of the argument has reasonable advocates who speak for the public interest. Minimum wage opponents argue the public interest is advanced through lower wages that help keep small businesses open and allow them to hire more workers. On the other hand, proponents argue that more money improves the welfare of poorer workers and circulates more money through the economy. Are small business owners acting against the public interest by opposing a higher minimum wage that might put them out of business? Are low-wage workers acting against the public interest by asking for more money that could improve their lives? Indeed, every area has many citizen groups that promote their interpretation of the public interest or the "national interest." When a group is making a normative claim for what might be called the "public good," the public interest is highly variable depending on who is defining it.

In the minimum wage example, how would you define the public interest? If you were a small business owner, you would likely define it in a very different way from a low-wage worker or a representative of a union. You might say that the public really has no clearly stated interest in setting wages, but they do display a preference for lower prices, and low prices have to come out of someone's earnings. Low-wage workers, on the other hand, might argue that more equality would benefit everyone, while higher prices might not be opposed and seem so bad if people at the bottom had enough money to pay them. These different arguments reflect the difficulty in defining a universal, agreed-upon public interest.

Public policy is related to the public interest because it affects all of us in some way. However, not everyone is necessarily affected by the same policy in exactly the same way. Nor is intensity of feeling about a particular issue necessarily equal among different members of the public. Most people care about their everyday lives but not too much about government because the activities of government seem removed from daily interests and needs. Still, the government plays an important role in every aspect of people's lives, from the power efficiency labeling on electrical appliances to registering and regulating hotels. As oppressive as government is claimed to be by some interests, at least some government activities are benign and beneficial to most people, and people tend not to dwell on those policies until something goes very wrong with them.

[Figure 1-2] The Government Role Extends to Hotels

You may be interested in public policy because you care intensely about a particular area of public policy—the economy, or the environment, or the promotion of morality and ethics in government. Even people who are intensely interested and are participants in the policy process are not concerned with every issue, though. There is considerable division of labor in democratic politics. Different positions have different constitutional responsibilities, and the vast array of issues that government handles on the people's behalf requires that even members of assemblies need to be specialists in fairly narrow fields.

The people delegate the power to make policies in their name (or, more precisely, the system is designed this way) because it is the people's government. The people cannot all be concerned with the day-to-day multitude of issues that government must address, so the people have delegated decision making to people who specialize in making the complex decisions that modern government must face. By delegating this power, the people do not abandon their interest in what the government does or how it does it (and sometimes the procedures government uses are at least as important as the goals to be achieved), nor do members of the public give up their right to promote their individual ideas of what constitutes the public interest.

3 A Look at the Study of Public Policy

Academics, policy analysts, and advocacy organizations, and citizen activists are not united by any single purpose. Instead, many interests move individuals and organizations to deal with public policy, and distinct aspects of its study reflect their interests. Academics, study public policy for scientific purposes. In other words, they work to build a general understanding of public problems and the policy–making process. They seek "truth" through scientific methods, regardless of whether the knowledge is relevant or useful in some immediate way. Their goal is to explain the causes and consequences of public policies, quite apart from what governments ought to do.

Some people study public policy for professional reasons, such as conducting policy analyses for government agencies, think tanks, or interest groups. Their objective is to examine public problems and policy alternatives and produce usable knowledge that can help policy makers, interest groups, or citizens choose those policies that are likely to achieve their desired outcomes.

Some analysts are committed to specific policy values and goals and sometimes to ideological and partisan agendas. Not surprisingly, they try to emphasize the studies and findings that help to advance their values and goals. This kind of policy study can be described as political, rather than professional or scientific.

Discussion Questions:

1. How would you define public policy?

2. How would you define the public interest? Can you give an example that conflicts with your definition?

3. What are the general reasons why people study public policy? Why are you studying it?

Vocabulary

public	*private actor*
private	*public interest*
public actor	*private interest*

References

Birkland, Thomas A. 2001. *An Introduction to the Policy Process: Theories, Concepts, and Models of Public Policy Making.* Armonk, New York: M. E. Sharpe.

Cochran, Clarke E., Mayer, Lawrence C., Carr, T. R., Cayer, N. Joseph, McKenzie, Mark J., and Peck, Laura R. 1999. *American Public Policy: An Introduction.* 6th ed. New York: St. Martin's Press.

Dye, Thomas R. 1992. *Understanding Public Policy.* 7th ed. Englewood Cliffs, New Jersey: Prentice Hall.

Gerston, Larry N. 2010. *Public Policy Making: Process and Principles.* Armonk, New York: M.E. Sharpe.

Kraft, Michael E. and Furlong, Scott R. 2004. *Public Policy: Politics, Analysis, and Alternatives.* Washington, D.C. CQ Press.

Peters, B. Guy. 1999. *American Public Policy: Promise and Performance.* Chappaqua, New York: Chatham House/Seven Rivers.

Sabatier, Paul A. 2007. "The Need for Better Theories," pp. 3-17 in Sabatier, Paul A. (ed), *Theories of the Policy Process,* 2nd ed. Boulder, CO: Westview Press.

Simon, Christopher A. 2009. *Public Policy: Preferences and Outcomes,* 2nd ed. New York, New York: Routledge.

"Seoul City to Lay Off 1,300 Officials." *English Chosun,* November 2, 2007, from http://english.chosun.com/w21data/html/news/200711/200711020018.html

WEEK 2 The Study of Public Policy

Summary

People study public policy for theoretical and academic scientific reasons. It is studied for political reasons, for more effective participation, and for better insight into choosing political candidates.

Public policy takes place in a social and cultural context. It is also affected by the political and governing context as well as by an economic context that is concerned with inflation and unemployment. Public policy is a response to market failure, and can include the provision of public goods, the addressing of externalities, the maintenance of natural monopolies, and the balancing of information asymmetries.

4 Why Do We Study Public Policy?

There are many different reasons to study public policy. They include theoretical reasons (Cochran et al., 1999) or scientific reasons (Anderson, 2000). Analysts, practitioners, and academics want to understand the theory in order to comprehend the public policy process. Understanding the theory can allow analysts and practitioners to apply theory for practical purposes. Academics use theory to help with scientific understanding.

Therefore people may study public policy in order to know more about the process both in pursuit of knowledge for its own sake and to inform practitioners. This is a question of so-called "pure" science versus "applied" science. Scholars at universities and in research institutes also have some of the same interests as policy analysts, but scholars are more often concerned with building general knowledge of the policy process instead of affecting the process more directly. This is more related to pure science, of knowledge for its own sake.

Examples of applied science include using the science for practical political reasons, for more efficient participation, or for facilitating the democratic process by selecting candidates wisely.

Political Reasons

People with political goals study public policy so as to learn about how to promote the policy options that they prefer. Their purpose is to advance their political interests through the policy process. One group of people using knowledge of public policy for political purposes is the policy analyst. Policy analysts work inside and outside of government to understand and influence policy. Therefore, they have a professional concern for public policy as part of their job.

Another group of people interested in policy for political purposes is made up of concerned citizens. For citizens, strong personal interest by itself should be a good reason to study public policy. Studying public policy may help citizens:

- sharpen their skills
- decide what political positions and policies to support
- evaluate democratic governance.

It may also encourage students to consider and/or to prepare for careers in public policy, law, or government.

More Efficient Participation

In a democracy, citizens choose representatives to act on their behalf, but that is not the last step of citizen participation. Citizens may speak out during the policy development process and in response to government actions. People are not usually restrained by a lack of knowledge about public problems, policies, government decisions, or politics. However, they can participate more effectively and have greater leverage by improving their understanding of these issues.

Selecting Candidates Wisely

Candidates for public office state their positions on the issues during political campaigns. They do this through speeches and advertisements to persuade voters to support them. Voters who study public policy are better equipped to understand the candidates, their policy ideas, and are more prepared to evaluate them.

5 The Context of Public Policy

Public policy is affected by social and economic conditions.

In addition, the structure of government and national and local cultural norms are some of the variables that shape the policy process. As a result, a description of the context of public policy is important. Next is a discussion of the social, economic, political, governing, and cultural context of public policy.

[Figure 2-1] The Elderly Make Up the Fastest Growing Segment of the Korean Population

Social Context

Social conditions affect policy decisions in numerous ways, as is evident in controversies over phenomena as diverse as urban sprawl, internet privacy, and getting the economy going. Social conditions are dynamic and in a constant state of change although you may like to imagine society as unchanging. The population changes because of immigration, growth in non-traditional households, and lower or higher birth rates. These social changes alter how the public and policy makers view and act on problems ranging from crime to the rising cost of health care. The elderly currently make up the fastest growing segment of the Korean population. Their needs are different from the needs of the rest of the population, and they are more likely than younger citizens to demand that government pay attention to them.

Aging in Korea Unlike what you might expect, the provinces are aging more rapidly than the central metropolitan areas in Korea. *Chosun Ilbo* reports that South Jeolla Province will be more than 20% senior citizens by 2021. With the exception of heavily urbanized Gyeong-gi Province, the rest of the non-metropolitan part of the country will have more than 14% senior citizens with in the next eight years, with several provinces already having reached that point. This is not just an aging trend, but it is also a story of migration as the young people leave rural areas for the big cities. This migration has been so rapid that the trend in Seoul has been towards a much slower aging than in other areas. *English Chosun*

As the elderly population continues to increase, policy makers face difficult challenges. In particular, there is the question of how to ensure the pension system's solvency as greater numbers of people begin to draw benefits. In the past, the national pension system posed no special risk to budgetary resources. Public officials recognize that they must find politically and economically realistic ways of dealing with an aging population.

Other parts of the social context include the lower birth rate, the insecurity of forced early retirement, the increase in women in the workplace, as well as immigration (foreign workers in urban areas and large numbers of foreign wives in rural areas), and increasing emigration (Koreans moving to other countries and working and studying in other countries). All of these represent variables that can affect the policy-making process. How citizens relate to one another in their communities also influences public policy making.

Economic Context

The economy has a major impact on the policies governments adopt and implement. Economic policy deals with *inflation* and *unemployment*, but the economy itself affects the development of many other programs. For example, a strong economy often leads to lower unemployment, which, in turn, reduces the need for welfare and comparable assistance programs. The Korean shift to a less regulated economy featuring more transparency along with the growth of service and IT sectors has had and will continue to have many impacts on public policy.

Another way to appreciate the influence of the economic context is to consider unemployment. The market has led to lower employment in Korea, particularly among youth, women, and senior citizens. *Chosun Ilbo* cited a report by the Organization for Economic Cooperation and Development (OECD) that showed Korean youth unemployment at 10.0% in 2006 as compared to the OECD average of 14.7%. This has been a persistent problem as *JoongAng Ilbo* reported nine years later that youth employment had risen to 11.1%, the highest since statistics have been kept in their current form. Even though Korea's unemployment does not sound particularly high when compared to the OECD average, the youth unemployment figure only includes active members of the labor market. Youth labor market participation has remained very low, declining from a very low 40.5% in 2009 to an even lower 39.7% in 2015 (MOEL, 2015). Korean policy makers must be more sensitive to the issue of low youth employment than even the unemployment numbers would suggest. The low employment figure suggests that the issue is not one of too few jobs, but instead an issue of too few jobs that are good enough to lure young workers into the labor market to accept the jobs that are available.

Political Context

Politics affects public policy choices at every step, from the selection of policy makers in elections to shaping how conflicts among different groups are resolved. To appreciate the political context, one must be aware of the relative strength of the major parties. The influence of minor parties, the ideological differences among the public, especially the more attentive public groups such as committed liberals and conservatives. The ability of organized interest groups to exert pressure are also important factors.

Liberals and conservatives, regardless of the names of the current parties they belong to, often hold sharply different views about the legitimacy of government action and which policies are acceptable. Ideological polarization between the parties makes government action difficult on many policy issues. The student of public policy also needs to recognize that political labels such as liberal and conservative are not always a reliable guide to predicting specific policy positions.

It is simplistic to think that conservatives always want a smaller government and that liberals favor the opposite. Most conservatives argue against more government regulation of the economy and for decision making by business and industry.

They often also favor a strong government role in achieving certain social goals, such as maintaining the traditional social order. Liberals, on the other hand, tend to call for government regulation of business activity to protect consumers and workers or to control air and water pollution.

Party labels, may be a poor indicator of positions taken on policy issues, especially as party labels change so fast, with some politicians associated with different parties almost every election. Within the major political parties one can easily find ideological differences among members. For example, the New Politics Alliance for Democracy is a merger blending several strains of liberalism.

Sohn Hakgyoo was an assemblyman from the conservative New Korea Party, governor of Gyeong-gi Province and presidential primary candidate in the conservative Grand National Party (running against Lee Myungbak and Park Geunhye), and former leader of the liberal United Democratic Party. Moon Jae-in was Roh Moohyun's chief of staff, lost to President Park as the candidate of the United Democratic Party, and served as leader of NPAD. Ahn Chulsoo was a nonpartisan professor and businessman running for president in 2012 before he swung his support behind Moon Jae-in and then formed his own liberal New Political Vision Party that merged with the United Democrats to form the NPAD. The conservatives and minor parties also have similar complicated histories with numerous ideological divisions.

Governing Context

The government structure of a country has a major impact on public policy. Separation of powers requires that any policy developed at the national level be acceptable to a majority of the national assembly and to the president. Policy makers in both institutions must therefore find common ground.

Under the Korean political system, the national government shares some governing responsibilities with local governments. Prior to the beginning of local government autonomy in the 1990s, local governments were completely subordinate to the national government. The situation is less clear today. It is possible to have a president, such as Park Geunhye from one party, and to have a mayors like Park Wonsoon from the opposition pursuing policies in the opposite direction and without close coordination. In light of the complexity of the governance structure, with its overlapping responsibilities and political disagreements it might be accurate to say that it is amazing that policies get created and implemented at all.

Cultural Context

Political culture refers to widely held values, beliefs, and attitudes, such as trust and confidence in government and the political process, or the lack of it. Political cultures not only vary from nation to nation but from region to region within Korea, and even from one community to another, as one might expect in a modern society. These cultural differences help to explain the variation in provincial (and municipal) policies across the nation.

Different cities adopt different approaches to development, with Seoul under Mayor Park Wonsoon investing in people and welfare while many other Korean cities develop through investments in places like stadiums, housing, and parks. Policy makers in these different communities make different policy calculations on the basis of very different political cultures.

Cultural conflicts also affect public judgments about

government officials and their conduct and many influence the policy-making process. The reaction to Roh Moohyun's impeachment provoked a backlash that brought his party a large majority in the next election. Subsequent assessments of Roh Moohyun's presidential leadership led to his party's defeat in election after election and to the party's eventual disbanding. President Park Geunhye was attacked by critics of her father through her election campaign making it more difficult to pursue some of her policy priorities.

6 Market Failure: Rationale for Public Policy

In a market economy, private actors are supposed to provide for the needs of people. However, they are not always able to do so. Such market failure is a major rationale for government action. Four commonly recognized kinds of market failure include public goods, externalities, natural monopolies, and information asymmetries. They provide the traditional economic rationales for public participation in private affairs.

Public Goods

The terms *public goods* and *collective goods* appear frequently in the economics and policy analysis literature. The blanket use of the term, however, obscures important differences among the varieties of public goods. These differences include the nature of the market failure and, consequently, the appropriate public policy response. A basic question should be raised when considering any market failure, that is: Why does the market fail to allocate this particular good efficiently? The simplest approach to providing an answer involves contrasting public goods with private goods.

Two primary characteristics define private goods, rivalry in consumption and excludability in ownership and use. *Rivalrous consumption* means that when a thing is consumed it cannot be consumed by anyone else. A perfectly private good has complete consumption rivalry. *Excludable ownership* means that only one person or entity has control over the use of the good. A perfectly private good is completely excludable. For example, shoes are private goods because when one person wears them, no one else can wear them (rivalrous consumption) and the person who owns them can determine who gets to wear them at any particular time (excludable ownership).

Pure public goods, on the other hand, are either *non-rivalrous* in consumption, *non-excludable* in use, or both. In other words, any good that is not purely private is considered to be a public good. A good is non-rivalrous in consumption when more than one person can receive consumption benefits from some level of supply at the same time. For example, policing and national defense are non-rivalrous in consumption because all citizens benefit from them without reducing the benefits of others – a new citizen enjoys the same benefits without reducing the benefits of those already defended. A good is non-excludable if it is impractical for one person to maintain exclusive control over its use. For example, species of fish that range widely in the ocean are usually non-excludable in use because they move freely between national and international waters so that no individual can effectively exclude others from harvesting them.

[Figure 2-2] Policing is a Public Good

Externalities

An externality is any impact (positive or negative) resulting from any action (that may be related either to production or consumption) that affects someone who did not fully agree to it through participation in a voluntary exchange. Price changes in competitive markets are not relevant externalities because buyers and sellers engage in voluntary exchange by participating in the market. Pollution that hurts people who live near a factory and are exposed by chance is an example of a negative externality.

[Table 2-1] Examples of Externalities

	Positive	Negative
Producer-to-Producer	Recreational facilities attract people who purchase from nearby business	Toxic chemical pollution harms downstream commercial fishing
Producer-to-Consumer	Private timber forests provide scenic benefits to nature lovers	Factories pollute the air harming lungs of people living nearby
Consumer-to-Consumer	Immunization against contagious disease helps to reduce risk to others	Cigarette smoke hurts the health of non-smokers
Consumer-to-Producer	Letters from consumers providing information on product quality	Trespassers damaging private property by taking a shortcut

Natural Monopoly

Natural monopoly occurs when the average cost declines over the range of demand. This definition is in terms of both cost and demand conditions. In the case of a natural monopoly, a single firm can produce the output at a lower cost than can any other market arrangement, including competition. Even though the basic definition of a natural monopoly sounds static, markets in the real world are dynamic. Technological change may lead to different cost characteristics, or high prices may force the replacement of goods by close or even superior substitutes. The result may be the elimination of a natural monopoly or the supplanting of one natural monopoly technology by another. For example, cellular phones may be direct substitutes for line-connected phones, providing competition for traditional telephone systems.

Information Asymmetry

Information itself has the characteristics of a public good. Consumption of information is non-rivalrous. One person's consumption does not interfere with another's. The basic question is primarily whether exclusion is or is not possible. Thus the production and consumption itself is of interest in the public goods context. Second, there may be situations where the amount of information about the characteristics of a good varies between people. The buyer and the seller in a market transaction, for example, may have different information about the quality of the good being traded. Similarly, there may be differences in the level of information relating to the attributes of an externality between the generator of the externality and the affected party. Workers, for instance, may not be as well informed about the health risks of industrial chemicals as their employers.

Traditional market failures indicate possibilities for improving the efficiency of market outcomes through collective action. Market failures and unsatisfied distributional goals are necessary but not sufficient grounds for public intervention. The costs of the proposed intervention must always be considered. Just as markets fail in fairly predictable ways, government failures may contribute to the costs of policy interventions. They may also be a cause of policy failure.

Discussion Questions:

1. Why are you studying public policy? How are your professor's motivations similar to or different from yours?

2. How can the study of public policy improve government

and the democratic political process?

3. How can the study of public policy be useful?

4. Identify and explain the different policy contexts.

5. Identify and explain the different types of market failure.

6. Give examples of public and private goods and explain how they differ.

Vocabulary

inflation	*rivalrous consumption*
unemployment	*excludable ownership*
public goods	*non-rivalrous consumption*
collective goods	*non-excludable ownership*

References

"Aging Society Starts in the Provinces." *English Chosun,* April 26, 2005, from http://english.chosun.com/w21data/html/news/200504/200504260021.html

Anderson, James E. 2000. *Public Policy Making.* 4th ed. Boston: Houghton Mifflin.

Birkland, Thomas A. 2001. *An Introduction to the Policy Process: Theories, Concepts, and Models of Public Policy Making.* New York: M. E. Sharpe.

Cochran, Clarke E., Mayer, Lawrence C., Carr, T. R., Cayer, N. Joseph, McKenzie, Mark J., and Peck, Laura R. 1999. *American Public Policy: An Introduction.* 6th ed. New York: St. Martin's Press.

Elazar, Daniel J. 1984. *American Federalism: A View from the States.* 3rd ed. New York: Harper and Row.

Kim, Heejin. 2015. "Jobless Rate for Young Koreans Rises to 11.1%." *Korea JoongAng Daily.* March 19, 2015 from http://koreajoongangdaily.joins.com/news/article/Article.aspx?aid=3002087

Kraft, Michael E., and Furlong, Scott R. 2004. *Public Policy: Politics, Analysis, and Alternatives.* Washington, D.C. CQ Press.

Mazmanian, Daniel A., and Kraft, Michael E. eds. 1999. *Toward Sustainable Communities: Transition and Transformations in Environmental Policy.* Cambridge: MIT Press.

MOEL(Ministry of Employment and Labor). 2015. "Major Statistics," August 10, 2015, from http://www.moel.go.kr/english/pas/pasMajor.jsp

Putnam, Robert D. 1995. "Tuning In, Tuning Out: The Strange Disappearance of Social Capital in America." *PS: Political Science and Politics,* 28 (December): 664-683.

Weimer, L. David and Vining, R. Aidan. 2005. *Policy Analysis: Concept and Practice.* 4th ed. Upper Saddle River, New Jersey.

"Youth Unemployment in Korea on the Rise." *English Chosun,* December 24, 2007, from http://english.chosun.com/w21data/html/news/200712/200712240012.html

WEEK 3 Actors and Their Roles in Public Policy

Summary

There are official and unofficial actors in the public policy process. Official actors belong to parts of the government. The legislature, consisting of the national and local assemblies, passes laws, conducts oversight, and engages in casework for constituents. The executive, consisting of the president, governors, and mayors, carries out the law and uses executive bodies to advance policy. The executive also has access to the media and can do a lot to set the national/local agenda. Administrative agencies and bureaucracies carry out law, make regulations, and interpret legal provisions. The courts judge the law in action, with the Constitutional Court deciding the constitutionality of laws.

Unofficial actors include individual citizens, interest groups, and think tanks. All of them can influence the direction of policy. Much of the actions of government are organized within the political parties. The media have great influence over the direction of the public policy agenda.

The players in the public policy process are divided into two main categories:

- Official Actors
- Unofficial Actors

Official actors are involved in public policy by virtue of their statutory or constitutional responsibilities and have the power to make and enforce policies. The legislative, executive, and judicial branches are clearly official institutions. Unofficial actors include those who play a role in the policy process without any explicit legal authority (or duty) to participate, aside from the usual rights of participants in a democracy. Thus interest groups are involved in politics not because they are sanctioned by law, but because interest groups are an effective way for people to express their collective desires for policy. The media have rights to freedom of the press because of their implicit roles as provider of political information and as watchdogs over government, but the news media have no formal guaranteed role in policy making. Under certain conditions, such as matters of national security, obscenity, or personal privacy, the media can be denied access to policy making information and processes.

7 Official Actors and Roles

The Legislative Branch

The legislative branch is the subject of a lot of research as political scientists continue to work to understand how the legislature works and why it does what it does. In the Republic of Korea, the National Assembly plays the role of the national legislature.

What does a legislature do? The very name of this branch suggests lawmaking, and this is assumed to be the primary function of the legislative branch. In fact, though, according to the web site of the National Assembly of the Republic of Korea, the constitution gives the assembly three broad powers. These include legislative power, fiscal power, and oversight power over the national administration.

Legislative power includes the right to propose and decide upon putting up amendments to the constitution to a public referendum. It also includes the right to reject or to agree to and ratify foreign treaties. Finally, it includes the lawmaking function implied in the name legislature that is assumed to be the main job of the assembly.

Fiscal power is the second power vested in the national assembly. It includes the right to deliberate and settle budget bills, deliberate and settle accounts and funds, and the legislative right to finance. The assembly decides on the form and size of taxes.

The final power is oversight over national administration. This means that the assembly may inspect and investigate the national administration. It may also impeach the president, the prime minister, members of the State Council, heads of executive ministries, justices of the Constitutional Court, judges and members of the National Election Commission, members of the Board of Audit and Inspection and other public officials designated by law who have violated the Constitution or other laws. Short of impeachment, the assembly may pass a recommendation for the removal of the prime minister or a member of the State Council from office. Finally, in pursuit of oversight, the assembly may request that the prime minister, members of the State Council, or government representatives attend the assembly and answer questions.

The Executive Branch

When people think about "administration" they tend to think of the president, his immediate staff, and appointees. This is the sense in which the executive branch will be discussed. The president has some considerable advantages in policy making when compared with the legislature.

The president enjoys considerable organizational advantages over the assembly. The presidency is a unitary branch of government, in that it has the president at its head and a staff (or at least, most of the staff) that works for him or her in pursuit of the administration's goals. The assembly is divided into different parties with different interests, whereas everyone in the executive branch−the prime minister, members of the State Council, and the various ministers are all chosen by and accountable to the president.

By the nature of his or her high profile as head of state and head of government, the president receives a great amount of media and public attention. In these two roles, the president symbolizes and represents Korea both domestically and worldwide. Wherever the president goes, he or she is an important focus of media attention.

An important advantage the president enjoys is his or her informational advantage over the legislative branch. For decades, the executive branch has had access to the most information about government: what is being done, how much is actually being spent, as well as the nature and cause of public problems. Indeed, Cheongwadae, the Korean equivalent of the

White House, is a very large organization unto itself.

[Figure 3-1] Cheongwadae, the Blue House, Korea's White House

The presidency is particularly interesting to policy scholars because of the executive's role in policy making. The president is more involved with agenda setting than in developing policy alternatives to address the issues and problems. It is easy for the president to use his or her position to bring issues to the policy agenda and to push his or her preferred policy options once they are there. This is due in large part to the president's position in the public and to the office's constitutional responsibilities.

Bureaucrats and Administrative Agencies

In simple terms, government agencies provide services that are uneconomical for the private sector to provide directly, or they carry out the tasks that the people demand from government but have chosen not to ask the private sector to provide. In general, any good that carries with it major free-rider problems is a public good (see the previous chapter for a discussion of public goods). Public goods are goods that are indivisible (non-rivalrous) and non-exclusive (non-excludable).

These administrative agencies and bureaucrats are part of the national civil service and are employed by and accountable to the executive branch although the legislative branch does have oversight powers over the bureaucracy.

The Courts

The Korean judiciary is divided between a Supreme Court and a Constitutional Court. The Supreme Court is the highest court of appeals in the Korean legal system. The Constitutional Court judges the legality of legislation and government acts as judged against the standard of the National Constitution of the Republic of Korea. It was the Constitutional Court that decided that the National Assembly had acted improperly when it impeached and removed President Roh Moohyun from office. The Constitutional Court was also responsible for overturning the law that made adultery illegal. The Constitutional Court has the clearest role in the policy process.

What role has the court played in public policy making? In a long accepted practice, most public policy scholars have divided the courts from the other branches under the notion of separating law from politics. Woodrow Wilson (1887) argued that the American Congress makes public policy and the bureaucracy simply carries out that policy without exercising discretion. In making this argument, Wilson implicitly embraced the notion that courts cannot be policy makers because they are engaged in the neutral discovery of legal principles. Where the legislature is identified with compromise and the exchange of votes in the pursuit of policy preferences, the legal system is identified with the pursuit of more abstract principles, such as justice, associated with the notion of law. Thus, the Wilsonian perspective established a distinction between law and politics in relation to policy making. Politics created policy, and the law ensured that such policy was implemented justly.

While the simplicity of the Wilsonian perspective has long since been rejected, subsequent public policy theories have accepted, without serious question, his implicit distinction between law and institutions as structured by the constitutional order. In this context, the Constitutional Court determines the boundaries of policy making by the other branches, but these boundaries are claimed to have been created neutrally. That is, they are made without consideration for or the involvement of policy making. The court is assumed not to be engaged in policy making when it sets the boundaries of acceptable policy. It is simply engaged in the practice of articulating a socially-accepted and predetermined set of rules. In this way, the court is simply discovering or clarifying rules that we, as a society, have previously agreed to follow.

Even the everyday act of resolving disputes requires the courts to determine the acceptable application of many policies. As Edward Levi (1949) notes, the bargaining process inherent in legislatures and the uncertainty as to all possible future applications often requires elected officials to be purposely vague in the drafting laws. This fact means the Constitutional Court is required to make choices in the application of laws to new situations or to fine-tune laws to ensure their successful application in the real world. Thus, legislatures and executives initiate public policy, while the court reacts to the practical effects of such policies. These choices in determining the outcome of the policies in the real world act to further draw the courts into policy making.

8 Unofficial Actors and Roles

Unofficial actors indicate those actors who are not official because their participation in the policy process is not a function of their duties under the constitution or the law. This is not to say that these actors have no legal rights or standing to participate in the process; rather it means that their mode of participation is not specified in law. These unofficial actors include:

- Individual citizens
- Interest groups
- Political parties
- Think tanks and other research organizations
- Communications media

Individual Citizens

How do individuals play a role in policy making? If one believes in broad-based political participation as a key feature of democracy, it may be heartening to realize that people have been and can be mobilized. In other words, anyone can be persuaded to care about particular issues. Non-voters and relatively uninterested people can still be sufficiently motivated to join an interest group or take other political actions. People will often act when something threatens, or appears to threaten, their livelihood or their lifestyle, such as when commercial development disturbs their neighborhood, or when government is unresponsive to local needs for education or public safety. While some people will mobilize to try to get the government to do something about a problem, other people will often organize to get the government not to do something—not to approve a new waste dump, not allow obscene material on the internet, not allow unethical political campaigning. The decision not to approve a program or not to do something is as much a policy as is the decision to act affirmatively to do something, and it is often true that blocking an action is more easily achieved than actually moving a policy idea forward.

Interest Groups

Interest groups are made up of a number of individuals sharing a common purpose. A social movement is created when interest groups come together and create broader demands for change. A social movement involves far more people – although not all at a higher degree of activity than the membership of relevant interest groups. Social movements often involve a coalition of groups with similar goals, while other people support movements without a formal group affiliation. However, there are many ways to categorize interest groups. An institutional interest group, whose members belong to a particular institution can be distinguished from a membership group, whose members have chosen to join. If you are a student at a university, you are a member of an institutional interest group, university students, because you share some interests with your fellow students, such as affordable tuition and quality education. If you join an NGO, you are part of a membership group because you have chosen to join. Interest groups can also be categorized as economic or private interest groups versus public interest groups. Public interest groups, such as environmental groups, seek to create broad benefits for the society, not simply for their members.

[Figure 3-2] An Interest Group Protests

Interest groups engage in a range of activities to make their voices heard. Many groups engage in lobbying elected and appointed officials. The term lobbying has a negative connotation because of the well-known unethical actions of some private interests in influencing elected and unelected officials. However, lobbying is a neutral term for exercising influence. Protests are a way of exercising influence in public.

Political Parties

Political parties serve important functions in the policy process. First, party labels provide voters with cues for voting. Voters know, in general, that the Democratic Party tends to be a more socially liberal party. Second, political parties provide a way for the electorate to transmit rough political preferences to the elected branches of government. Third, political parties help elected officials and their supporters create packages of policy ideas that can be used to appeal to voters and then shaped into legislation. Finally, political parties are crucial to organization of the legislative branch. National and local assemblies elect their leadership along party lines, and committee assignments are made based on party.

Think Tanks and Other Research Organizations

The development of more complex government problems and the need for greater analytical ability have led to the growth of independent research organizations, or what are

[Figure 3-3] *Seoul Newspaper* and the Korea Press Center Watch over Seoul City Hall, along with *DongA Daily* and Other Media

often called think tanks. Research organizations and think tanks can provide valuable input into the policy process.

Communications Media

The news media are important actors in the policy process. Indeed, the freedom of the press (which today includes radio, television, the Internet, and other new media) provides for a vigorous, activist press that serves as a "watchdog" over government. Journalists and academics have reinforced the belief that the news media play an important role in informing citizens about issues and what their government is doing about them. There are many historic examples of the media exposing some of the troubling activities and shortcomings of business and government.

The Korean media were roundly criticized for failing in this watchdog role in the case of the Sewol ferry disaster. In particular, the media came under fire for uncritically accepting inconsistent and inaccurate government announcements while intruding on the privacy of grieving families still in shock over their loss (see box below).

Newspapers remain important to policy elites and to some mass audiences. Many are widely read in policy making circles. In addition, their audience is multiplied over the web. Free newspapers distributed in subways are another new press outlet. Television is the primary source of news for most Koreans who consume news. The particular importance of the media is in its agenda-setting function. They help elevate some issues to greater public attention.

Watchdogs Not Barking April 16, 2014 the ferry MV Sewol capsized, claiming the lives of 304 passengers and crew, including a large number of high school students on a field trip. Journalists covering the disaster came under criticism for a variety of ethical breaches, including harassing victims' families, taking photographs without permission, and even breaking into the high school so many of the young victims attended. Seen as insensitive and abrasive towards victims, the media were often also criticized for failing to question the government's information while publishing uncritical reports that did not search aggressively for the truth or even check many of the basic facts. Park Chongryul, president of the Journalists Association of Korea, rhetorically asked whether the sensational reporting was really necessary in an interview with *The Korea Herald.* He stressed that "The public wanted to know what really happened, not what the government says." In the wake of the criticism, Park said that reporters should apologize and realize that, in a digital age, they are being watched and will be held immediately to account for failing the public. Park helped craft a set of non-binding rules for journalists to follow when covering future disasters in the hope of giving the watchdog media back its bark. *The Korea Herald*

Discussion Questions:

1. What are the differences between official and unofficial actors? Give examples of each.
2. What are the three branches of government? What are their powers in Korea?

3. What are the two high courts in Korea? What are their policy roles?

4. What are some ways citizens can get involved in the policy process? How have you participated?

5. Which official and unofficial actors have the most power to set the agenda?

6. What are the advantages of political parties?

7. What are some problems with the exercise of influence by different unofficial actors?

Vocabulary

official actors
unofficial actors
legislative
executive
judicial
National Assembly
Constitutional Court
individual citizens
interest groups
political parties
think tanks
research organizations
communication media

References

Birkland, Thomas A. 2001. *An Introduction to the Policy Process: Theories, Concepts, and Models of Public Policy Making*. New York: M. E. Sharpe.

Cho, Chung-un. 2014. "Sewol Disaster Reveals Failure of Mass Media as Watchdog." *Korea Herald*, May 16, 2014 from http://www.koreaherald.com/view.php?ud=20140516001217

Choe, Sanghyun. 2015. "Adultery is No Longer an Affair of the State in South Korea," February 26, 2015 from http://www.nytimes.com/2015/02/27/world/asia/south-korea-strikes-down-adultery-law.html

"Constitution of the Republic of Korea" from http://korea.na.go.kr/-res/low_01_read.jsp

Kingdon, John W. 1995. *Agendas, Alternatives and Public Policies*. 2nd ed. New York: Harper Collins.

Kraft, Michael E. and Furlong, Scott R. 2004. *Public Policy: Politics, Analysis, and Alternatives*. Washington, D.C.: CQ Press.

Levi, Edward. 1949. *An Introduction to Legal Reasoning*. Chicago: University of Chicago Press.

Olson, Mancur. 1971. *The Logic of Collective Action*. Cambridge: Harvard University Press.

"Powers of the National Assembly" from http://korea.na.go.kr/int/aut_01.jsp?leftid=CA

Ripley, Randall and Franklin, Grace. 1991. *Congress, the Bureaucracy and Public Policy*. 5th ed. Pacific Grove, California: Brooks-Cole.

Wilson, Woodrow. 1887. "The Study of Administration," pp. 22-37, in Shafritz, Jay, Hyde, Alan, and Parkes, Sandra (eds). 2004. *Classics of Public Administration*, 5th ed. Belmont, California: Wadsworth.

Wood, B. Dan. 1991. "Federalism and Policy Responsiveness: The Clean Air Case." *Journal of Politics*, 53 (3): 851-859.

WEEK 4 Models and Theories

Summary

Social scientists use models that are abstract representations of how things work.

Elite theory says that there is a divide between the few with power and the many without. The few are not typical, have a consensus, and their values are reflected in public policy. Active elites are not greatly influenced by the masses, although there are different elites and different elite actors. Group theory is associated with pluralism. It says that policy is the product of continuous struggle among organized groups. Institutional theory emphasizes the formal, legal aspects of government structure. Rational choice, also known as public choice or formal theory, uses economics, and mathematical modeling. Public choice is the consideration of individual valuation in pursuit of self-interest. Political systems theory looks at the operation of the political system in terms of inputs, environmental demands, policy outputs and outcomes, and feedback. The policy process model looks at the logical sequence of activities affecting policy development, through the stream metaphor, advocacy coalition framework, and punctuated equilibrium.

9 Policy Theories: Elite, Group, Institutional, Rational Choice, and Political System Theories

Social scientists use models and theories that are abstract representations of the real world, to understand the way things work. Policy scientists use several different models and theories for policy making. The most common theories are:

- Elite theory
- Group theory
- Institutional theory
- Rational choice theory
- Political system theory

Elite Theory

Elite theory suggests that a relatively few people in key positions in government, industry, academia, the media, and other institutions control a disproportionate share of the nation's economic and political resources. Policy is dominated by the best educated, wealthiest, and most powerful elites. This is the principal belief of elite theory.

Elite theory emphasizes how the values and preferences of governing elites, which may differ from those of the public at large, affect public policy development. The primary assumption of this theory is that the values and preferences of the general public are less influential in shaping public policy than those of a smaller unrepresentative group of people, or elites. Elite theory suggests that the people are apathetic and ill-informed about public policy, that elites actually shape mass opinion on policy questions more than masses shape elite opinion.

The Elite Model can be summarized briefly as follows:

- Society is divided into the few who have power and the many who do not. Only a small number of people allocate values for society. The masses do not decide public policy.
- The few who govern are not typical of the masses who are governed. Elites are drawn disproportionately from the upper socioeconomic strata of society.

[Figure 4-1] The Elite Model

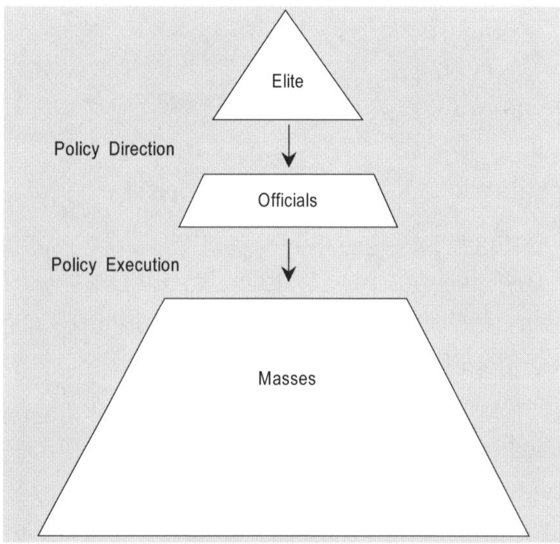

- The movement of non-elites to elite positions must be slow and continuous to maintain stability and avoid revolution. Only non-elites who have accepted the basic elite consensus can be admitted to governing circles.
- Elites share a consensus on behalf of the basic values of the social system and the preservation of the system. In Korea, the bases of elite consensus include a market

orientation with a popular democratic political system organized along a liberal/conservative divide, a close relationship with the US, and a strong military based on universal conscription.

- Public policy does not reflect the demands of masses but rather the prevailing values of the elite. Changes in public policy will be incremental rather than revolutionary.
- Active elites are subject to relatively little direct influence from apathetic masses. Elites influence masses more than masses influence elites.

Policy actors according to elite theory. Policy actors may be economic elites – *chaebols*, wealthy people, corporate executives, and professionals such as physicians and attorneys (see box below). They may be cultural elites, such as actors, filmmakers, recording artists, and media stars. Elected officials constitute an elite, as do other influential policy actors, such as scientists and policy analysts. Elite theory, then, focuses on the role of leaders and leadership in the development of public policy.

A single power elite or establishment is seldom at the center of policy decisions because different policy elites tend to dominate in different policy areas. The role of different elites is particularly evident in sub-governments or issue networks. Elites can sometimes exert their influence through a process of symbolic politics. Policy makers often formulate public policies that appear to meet public needs but actually serve the material needs of narrow elites. The benefits conveyed to the public are largely symbolic.

A major shortcoming of elite theory is that some interests simply accept their fate and give elite groups relatively little trouble. Related to this is the assumption that the elite is somehow united, single-mindedly marching toward the same class-oriented goals.

More Influence, More Attention Lotte Group Chairman Shin Dongbin made an apology for the very public struggle for control of South Korea's retail giant, *The Straights Times* reported. Shin squabbled in 2015 in a family feud with his brother and his father who had founded the company 67 years before. Unlike most family fights, the power and influence of the Shin family through their ownership of the Lotte Group brought celebrity status and widespread media coverage to their fight. The Financial Consumer Agency, one of Korea's major consumer groups, called for a boycott of Lotte on August 4, 2015 over the intense family fight to highlight the excessive power that a few families exercise over mammoth conglomerate *chaebol* in Korea. Lotte got the message and Shin offered his apology one week later. Shin promised transparency, saying, "The current dispute has occurred as we have failed to make efforts to improve corporate governance and enhance transparency" and promised, "We will be bold in reform in order to address concerns held by the people of Korea, our shareholders, contractors and employees." Specific promises included public listing of Lotte Hotel at the center of the group followed by enhanced efforts at transparency. Whether or not the reforms would be faithfully carried out and the Korean public would accept them as enough, the family at the center of Lotte Group would continue to wield disproportionate influence in Korean business, society, and politics. *The Straights Times, English Chosun*

Group Theory

Group theory, closely associated with pluralism, sees public policy as the product of a continuous struggle among organized interest groups. Pluralists believe that power in the political system is widely shared among interest groups, each of which seeks access to the policy making process. Some groups provide countervailing power to others as they lobby legislators and executive officials and appeal to the broader public through issue-advocacy campaigns. For example, labor unions work to balance the influence of manufacturing interests.

This is one kind of balance that helps to ensure that no single group dominates the policy process. Even so, it is logical to assume that groups with greater financial resources, recognition, prestige, and access to policy makers are likely to have more influence than others. The poor and homeless are not well organized, lack significant political resources, and are poorly represented in the policy process. When people speak of "special interests" influencing government decisions, they are using the concept of group theory.

Group theory tends to exaggerate the role and influence of organized interest groups over policy and to underestimate the leadership of public officials and the considerable discretion they have in making policy choices. Hiding behind every policy decision is a special interest group eager to have its way, but assigning too much power to organized groups oversimplifies a more complex policy dynamic. Public officials also frequently use organized interest groups to promote their own political agendas and build support for policy initiatives. The relationship between groups and policy makers is often a subtle, two-way exercise of influence.

According to group theorists, public policy at any given time is the equilibrium reached in a group struggle (Figure 4-2). This equilibrium is determined by the relative influence of any interest group. Changes in the relative influence of interest groups can be expected to result in changes in public policy. Policy will move in the direction desired by the groups gaining influence and away from the desires of groups losing influence. The influence of groups is determined by their numbers, wealth, organizational strength, leadership, access to decision makers, and internal cohesion.

The whole interest group system is held together as part of the political system in equilibrium by several forces. First, there is a large group that supports the constitutional system and the prevailing rules of the game. This group is not always visible but can be activated to administer overwhelming rebuke to any group that attacks the system and threatens to destroy the equilibrium.

Second, overlapping group membership helps to maintain the equilibrium by preventing any one group from moving too far from prevailing values. Individuals who belong to any one group also belong to other groups, and this fact moderates the

[Figure 4-2] The Group Model

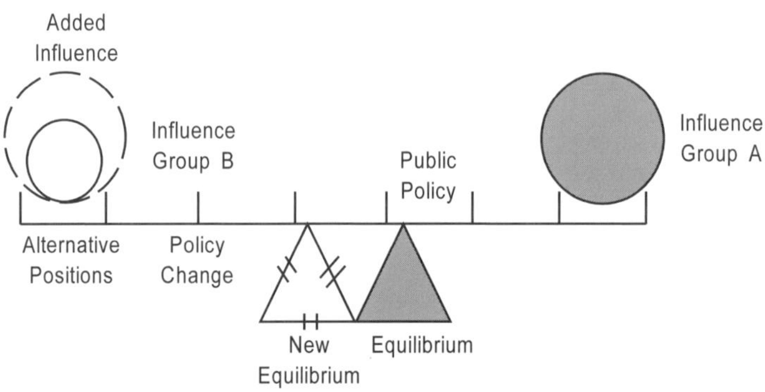

demands of groups who must avoid offending their members who have other group affiliations.

Finally, the balance resulting from group competition also helps to maintain equilibrium in the system. No single group constitutes an absolute majority on all questions. The power of each group is checked by the power of competing groups. Countervailing centers of power function to check the influence of any single group and protect individuals from exploitation.

Institutional Theory

Institutional theory emphasizes the formal and legal aspects of government structure. Institutional models look at the way governments are arranged, their legal powers, and their rules and procedures. Those rules include basic characteristics such

[Figure 4-3] Business Institutions Influence Public Policy

as the degree of access to decision making provided to the public, the availability of information from government agencies, and the sharing of authority between national and local governments. The term *institution* refers to both the organizations and the rules used to structure patterns of interaction within and across organizations. Many kinds of institutions can influence public policy: *markets, individual firms/corporations/-chaebol, national* and *local governments, voluntary associations* such as *political parties* and *interest groups,* and *foreign political regimes.*

Rational Choice Theory

Rational choice theory, also called public choice and formal theory, draws heavily on economics, especially microeconomic theory, and often uses elaborate mathematical modeling. Rational choice theory has been widely applied to questions of public policy. Analysts have used this theory to explain actions as diverse as individual voter decisions and the calculations of public officials as they face national security threats. It assumes that individuals are rational actors when making decisions.

Rational choice theory suggests that analysts consider what individuals value, how they perceive a given situation, the information they have about it, various uncertainties that might affect the outcome, and how a particular context or the expectations of others (rules and norms) might affect their actions. This theory tries to explain public policy in terms of the actions of individual self-interested policy actors, whether they are voters, corporate lobbyists, agency officials, or legislators. Public choice theory forces people to think about the core motivation of individual political actors and the consequences of such motivations for public policy and the larger political system.

This provides useful insights into political behavior that can affect the design of public policies. It is especially useful to formulate predictions of how agency officials and those who are the objects or targets of the policy are likely to respond to policy initiatives.

In order to select a rational policy, policy makers must: (1) know society's value preferences and their relative weights; (2) know all the policy alternatives available; (3) know all the consequences of each policy alternative; (4) calculate the ratio of benefits to costs for each policy alternative; and (5) select the most efficient policy alternative. This rationality assumes that the value preferences of society as a whole can be known and weighed. It is not enough to know and weigh the values of some groups and not others. There must be a complete understanding of societal values.

Rational policy making also requires information about alternate policies. It also requires the intelligence to calculate the ratio of costs to benefits accurately. Finally, rational policy making requires a decision-making system that facilitates rationality in policy formation. A diagram of such a system is shown in Figure 4-4.

Critics of public choice theory argue that individuals do not always pursue their own self-interest. The critics also question the narrow and rigid assumptions that underlie the theory. In addition, there are many barriers to rational decision making. Several important obstacles to rational policy making can be identified:

– No societal benefits are really agreed on-just benefits to specific groups and individuals, many of which are conflicting.

- Many conflicting benefits and costs cannot be compared or weighted. For example, it is impossible to compare or weight the value of individual dignity against a tax increase.
- Policy makers are not motivated to make decisions on the basis of societal goals but instead try to maximize their own rewards, such as power, status, re-election, and money.
- Policy makers are not motivated to maximize net social gain but merely to satisfy demands for progress. They do not search until they find "the one best way." Instead, they halt their search when they find an alternative that will work.

[Figure 4-4] A Rational Decision Model System

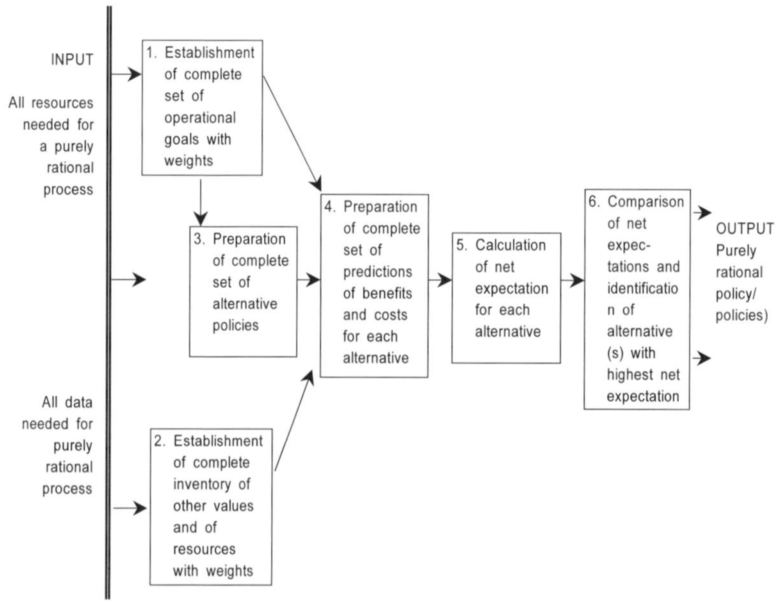

- Large investments in existing programs and policies (*sunk costs*) prevent policy makers from reconsidering alternatives now closed by previous decisions.
- There are innumerable barriers to collecting of the all information required to know all possible policy alternatives and the consequences of each. These include the cost of gathering information, the availability of information, and the time involved in data collection.
- Neither the predictive capacities of the social and behavioral sciences nor those of the physical and biological sciences are sufficiently advanced to enable policy makers to understand the full benefits or costs of each policy alternative.
- Policy makers do not have sufficient intelligence to calculate costs and benefits accurately even with the most advanced computerized analytical techniques. This is especially true when a large number of diverse political, social, economic, and cultural values are at stake.
- Uncertainty about the consequences of various policy alternatives compels policy makers to stick as closely as possible to previous policies to reduce the likelihood of unanticipated or disturbing consequences.
- The segmented nature of policy in large bureaucracies makes it difficult to coordinate decisions so that the input of all the various specialists is brought to bear at the point of making the final decision.

Political System Theory

Political system theory stresses the way the political system (the institutions and activities of government) responds to demands that arise from its environment, such as public opinion and interest group pressures. This theory emphasizes the larger social, economic, and cultural context in which political decisions and policy choices are made. Political system theory is a more formal way of thinking about the interrelationships between institutions and policy actors as well as the role of the larger environment. System theory also supplies some useful terms, such as *input, demands, support, policy outputs, policy outcomes,* and *feedback.*

Input into the political system comes from demands and support. Demands are the claims individuals and groups seeking to further their interests and values make on the political system. System theory is a simple way of portraying how governments respond to societal demands. It proposes an almost biological model of politics. It also suggests that governments and public officials react to the political climate like organisms respond to environmental stimuli (Katz and Kahn, 1966).

System theory portrays public policy as an output of the political system. The concept of "system" implies an identifiable set of institutions and activities in society that function to transform demands into authoritative decisions requiring the support of the whole society. The concept of system also implies that elements of the system are interrelated, that the system can respond to forces in its environment, and that it will do so to preserve itself. Inputs are received into the political system in the form of both demands and support. Support is when individuals or groups accept the outcome of elections, obey the laws, pay their taxes, and generally conform to policy decisions. Any system also absorbs a variety of demands, some of which conflict with each another.

The system must arrange and enforce settlements on the

parties concerned to transform these demands into outputs (public policies). It is recognized that outputs (public policies) may have a modifying effect on the environment and the demands arising from it, and they may also have an effect on the character of the political system. The system preserves itself by: (1) producing reasonably satisfying outputs; (2) relying on deeply-rooted attachments to the system itself; and (3) using or threatening to use force.

The value of the systems model to policy analysis lies in the questions that it poses:

- What are the significant dimensions of the environment that generate demands on the political system?
- What are the characteristics of the political system that enable it to change demands into policy to preserve itself over time?

Figure 4-5 shows the parts involved in system theory.

[Figure 4-5] The Systems Model

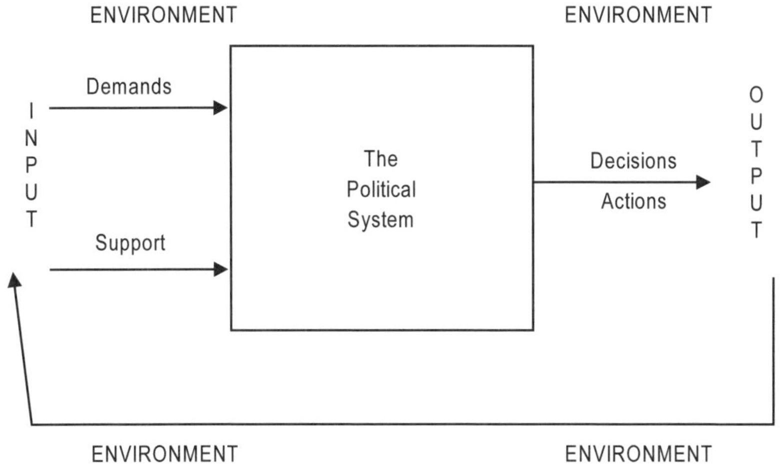

Each theory offers a different perspective on the principle determinants of decision making within government. Every theory suggests a distinct conceptual framework through which to view politics and public policy, highlighting particular features of the political and institutional landscape, though none is completely satisfactory by itself.

10 The Policy Process Model

A policy process model posits a logical sequence of activities affecting the development of public policies. It can also be helpful for understanding the flow of events and decisions in different cultures and institutional settings. The language and concepts are general enough to fit any political system and its policy process. Sometimes the phrase policy cycle is used to make clear that the process is cyclical or continuous rather than a one-time set of actions.

Any policy process model captures important aspects of

[Figure 4-6] The Streams Metaphor

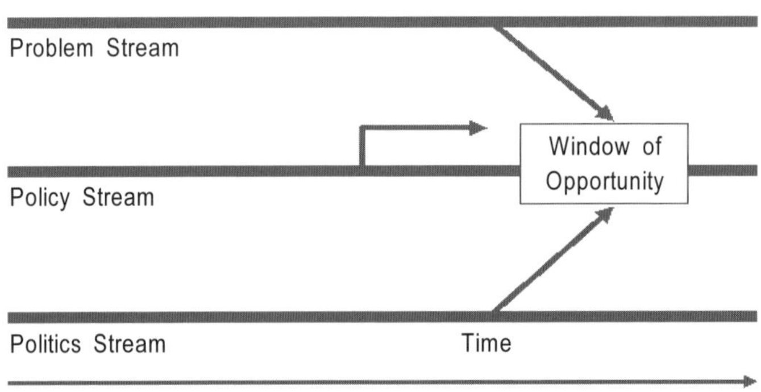

policy making that correspond to political reality. Here are three prominent recent models of the policy process:

- John Kingdon's "Streams metaphor"
- Paul Sabatier's "Advocacy coalition framework"
- Frank Baumgartner and Bryan Jones's "Punctuated equilibrium"

Streams Metaphor

Kingdon (1995) argues that issues gain agenda status and alternative solutions are selected when elements of three "streams" come together. Each of these three streams is associated with various individuals, groups, agencies, and institutions that are involved in the policy-making process. These three steams are (1) the *politics stream* that encompasses the state of politics and public opinion as well as (2) the *policy*

[Figure 4-7] Coalitions Come Together to Advocate Policy Preferences

stream, containing the potential solutions to a problem and (3) the *problem stream*, encompassing the attributes of a problem (Is it getting better or worse? Does it have a focusing event? Can it be solved with the alternatives available in the policy stream?). Figure 4-6 illustrates the streams metaphor.

The Advocacy Coalition Framework (ACF)

Sabatier's Advocacy Coalition Framework (ACF) (Sabatier, 1988) is an important model of the policy process, based on the idea that interest groups are organized into policy communities within a policy domain. The most recent version of this framework is depicted in Figure 4-8. In the ACF two to four advocacy coalitions typically form in a particular policy domain when groups come together around a shared set of core values and beliefs. These groups engage in policy debates, competing and compromising over solutions based on their core values and beliefs. Competition between coalitions is mediated by policy brokers who have a stake in resolving the problem, either on substantive grounds or because of their interest in maintaining political harmony in the system. These brokers are more likely to succeed when they can develop compromises that do not threaten either an advocacy coalition's core beliefs or values. Policy change is much less likely if polarization of advocacy coalitions is so great that there is no room on the periphery of the groups' belief systems where a compromise can be found.

Punctuated Equilibrium

Baumgartner and Jones (1993) argue that the balance of political power between groups of interests remains relatively stable over long periods of time, punctuated by relatively

[Figure 4-8] Advocacy Coalition Framework (ACF)

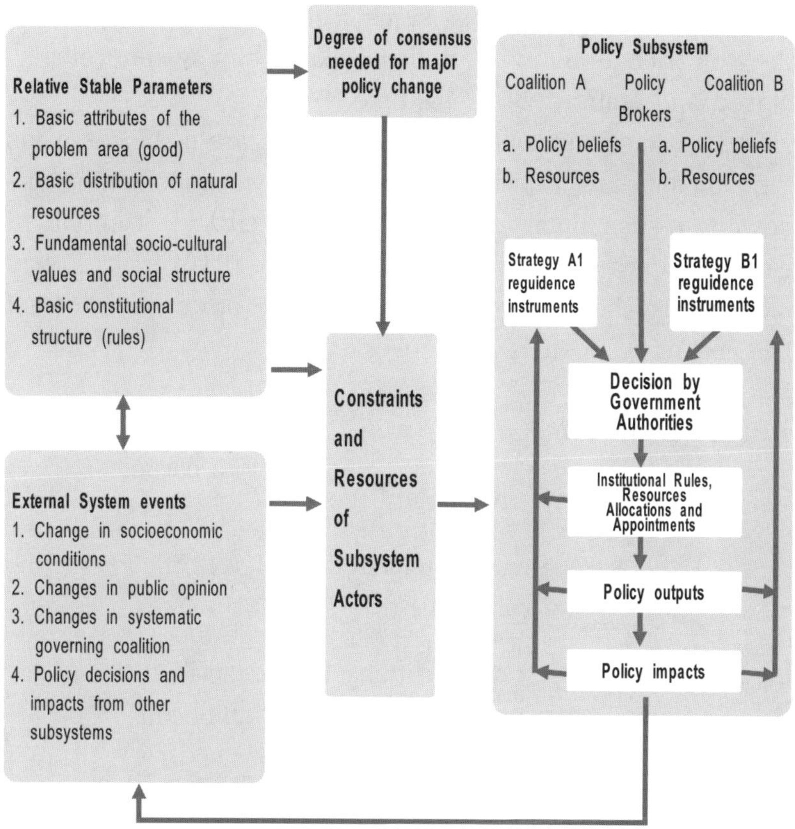

sudden shifts in public understanding of problems and in the balance of power between the groups seeking to fight entrenched interests.

Key to their theory of equilibrium is the idea of the *policy monopoly*. This corresponds with the idea of policy subsystems. A policy monopoly is a fairly concentrated, closed system of the most important policy making actors. Such a monopoly has an interest in keeping policy making closed, because a closed system benefits the interests of those in the monopoly and keeps policy making under some measure of control. Under the iron triangle notion of policy making, this system remains closed and stable for a long time.

Baumgartner and Jones argue that there are instances when the "equilibrium" maintained by policy monopolies breaks down. At such times greater and more critical attention to issues follows and rapid policy change is the result. Policy monopolies themselves can then break down or at least become more open issue networks.

Discussion Questions:

1. What are the five policy theories?
2. Who are the main actors in the different theories? Who plays those roles in Korea?
3. Which theory do you think best describes the policy process in Korea? Why do you think so?
4. What are the most important institutions in Korea?
5. What are the three policy streams? Give an example of a window of opportunity.
6. What is a Korean example of an advocacy coalition framework?
7. Give an example of a breakdown of a policy equilibrium in Korea. What happened to the policy monopoly?

Vocabulary

elite theory
group theory
institutional theory
rational choice theory
political system theory
cost/benefit analysis
sunk costs
input
demands
support
policy outputs
policy outcomes
feedback
streams metaphor
politics stream
policy stream
problem stream
window of opportunity
advocacy coalition
framework
punctuated equilibrium
policy monopoly

References

Baumgartner, Frank, and Jones, Bryan D. 1993. *Agendas and Instability in American Politics.* Chicago: University of Chicago Press.

Birkland, Thomas A. 2001. *An Introduction to the Policy Process.* New York: M.E. Sharpe.

"Boss of South Korea Retail Giant Lotte Apologises for Family Feud, Vows Reform." 2015. *The Straights Times*, August 11, 2015 from http://www.straitstimes.com/asia/east-asia/boss-of-south-korea-retail-giant-lotte-apologises-for-family-feud-vows-reform

Cochran, Clarke E., Mayer, Lawrence C., Carr, T. R., Cayer, N. Joseph, McKenzie, Mark J., and Peck, Laura R. 1999. *American Public Policy: An Introduction.* 6th ed. New York: St. Martin's Press.

"Consumer Groups Urge Lotte Boycott." 2015. *English Chosun*, August 5, 2015 from http://english.chosun.com/site/data/html_dir/2015/08/05/2015080501247.html

Dye, R. Thomas. 1995. *Understanding Public Policy.* 8th ed. Englewood Cliffs, New Jersey: Prentice Hall.

Katz, Daniel and Kahn, Robert L. 1966. "Organizations and the System Concept." pp. 206-216, in Shafritz, Jay, Hyde, Alan, and Parkes, Sandra (eds). 2004. *Classics of Public Administration,* 5th ed. Belmont, California: Wadsworth.

Kingdon, John W. 1995. *Agendas, Alternatives and Public Policies.* 2nd ed. New York: Harper Collins.

Kraft, Michael E. and Furlong, Scott R. 2004. *Public Policy: Politics, Analysis, and Alternatives.* Washington, D.C. CQ Press.

Lindblom, E. Charles. 1959. "The Science of Muddling Through." *Public Administration Review,* 19 (Spring): 79-88.

Sabatier, Paul A. 1988. "An Advocacy Coalition Framework of Policy Change and the Role of Policy-Oriented Learning Therein." *Policy Sciences,* 21: 129-168.

Wildavsky, Aaron. 1964. *The Politics of the Budgetary Process.* Boston: Little, Brown.

WEEK 5 Instruments and Types of Policy

Summary

The instruments of public policy include regulation, government management, taxing, spending, market mechanisms, education, information, and persuasion. Policy types include distributive, redistributive, as well as competitive and protective regulatory types.

11 Instruments of Public Policy

Policy makers consider many questions when deciding which policy instruments to use to address a particular issue or problem. The most obvious is whether the instrument will be effective in addressing the problem, but others include its political acceptability, technical feasibility, economic impact, and long-term effects. Some of the most common policy instruments are:

- Regulation
- Government management

- Taxing and spending
- Market mechanisms
- Education, information, and persuasion

Regulation

Regulation encompasses several different kinds of government actions, including the laws that legislatures enact and the rules bureaucracies adopt. Regulations are government decrees that either require citizens to do something or prevent them from doing something. Particular requirements ensure complaints by individuals, corporations, and other units of government. Typically, regulations impose sanctions, such as fines or imprisonment, for failure to comply. For the most part, citizens and corporations voluntarily comply with legal requirements, but means are available to force compliance when necessary.

Government Management

Government uses direct provision of services or the direct management of resources as instruments of public policy. Education, defense, public parks, and most municipal services are examples of policies that governments implement by providing services directly to citizens. Governments offer most of these services because they need to be provided in a specific way, such as making national park lands available to all for a modest fee. Today, it is not unusual for governments, especially at the local level, to contract out a wide variety of services and pay private companies to provide them.

Taxing and Spending

Governments use their ability to tax and spend to achieve policy goals and objectives. One form of spending policy is direct payment of money to citizens. Social welfare payments are an obvious example. The government transfers money from people who are working (taxpayers) to those who are covered by the system's rules. Governments also provide monetary payments as a way of promoting certain activities. For example, under American welfare reform, the federal government provides money to the state governments to distribute as they see fit to those needing assistance, but the states must show that they have reduced the number of people on welfare or risk losing some of this federal funding. Government spending policies affect a wide range of public activities, from scientific research to highway and mass transit construction as well as the protection of public lands.

Government also uses tax policy to promote or discourage certain activities. For example, the national government promotes insurance by allowing people who buy insurance to deduct their insurance payment from their taxable income when calculating their income tax. The government also tries to encourage consumption by allowing deductions for credit card and cash receipt expenditures.

Market Mechanisms

Governments can take advantage of market mechanisms as a form of public policy. Using the market may be an explicit decision by government not to intervene but instead to allow the laws of supply and demand to work. The federal government in the United States has chosen to favor online commerce by not extending any national taxation system to cover the buying and selling on the internet. This generally means that purchases pay and sellers collect retail sales tax only from purchases made online by customers in the same jurisdiction as the store. Online commerce is favored as local merchants doing business offline must charge and collect sales tax on all of their purchases and so operate at a disadvantage.

Governments also actively use market incentives rather than other approaches to achieve policy goals. For example, rather than providing some sort of national auto insurance, the Korean government encourages citizens to buy from private insurance companies.

Education, Information, and Persuasion

Citizen education is an instrument the government can use in an attempt to persuade people to behave in a certain way. Following the MERS outbreak, for example, the government instructed the public to report symptoms, take reasonable basic hygiene measures, and obey quarantine orders in order to prevent the spread of the disease. Likewise, the president will frequently make an appeal for public help following a national disaster such as a typhoon. This type of message is called exhortation or a hortatory appeal, and the president's authority can be an effective instrument of public policy under certain circumstances.

Providing information to the public can also be a powerful policy instrument. Some scholars call it a "capacity building" tool. It has the potential to inform, enlighten, and empower people through training, education, technical assistance, and making information available. Use of this instrument has increased in recent years and is common in the areas of health, safety, and environmental protection. For example, the Korea Food and Drug Administration requires nutritional labeling as a way of informing consumers about the substances in their food and allowing them to make decisions on healthy eating.

[Figure 5-1] President Roh Moohyun Persuaded the Public to Help after Typhoon Maemi

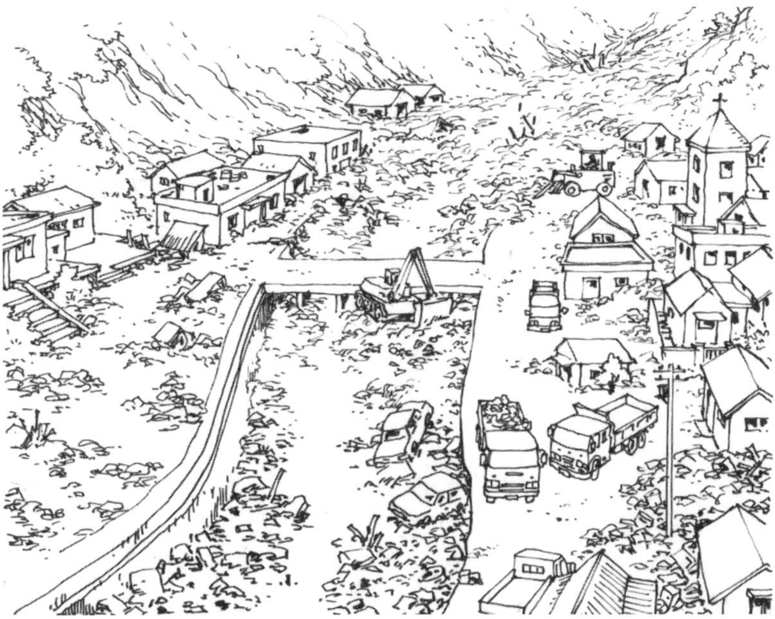

12 Policy Typologies

The earliest policy typologies generally separated policy into topical categories: education, health, or transportation, for example. This was useful for sorting different policy domains, but it did not help draw general conclusions about the politics that underlie these policies. On the other hand, Lowi (1964, 1979) described three types of policies on the basis of what they do. These include distributive, regulatory, and redistributive policy and are covered in this section.

[Table 5-1] Actors, Stability, and Visibility of Various Policy Types

Policy Type	Primary Actors	Relationships	Stability	Visibility
Distributive	Legislative subcommittees; executive bureaus; small interest groups	Logrolling (everyone gains)	Stable	Low
Protective regulatory	Legislative committees and subcommittees; full legislature; executive agencies; trade associations	Bargaining, compromise	Unstable	Moderate
Competitive regulatory	Legislative subcommittees; executive bureaus and commissions; small interest groups	Logrolling among favored actors	Stable	Very low
Redistributive	Executive and his appointees; committees and/or legislature; large interest groups; liberals/ conservatives	Ideological and class conflict	Stable	High

Distributive Policies

Distributive policies involve the granting of some sort of benefit to a particular interest group or other well-defined, relatively small group of beneficiaries. Examples of distributive policy include agricultural subsidies and national spending on local infrastructure projects. The creation of a new administrative capitol is a distributive policy benefitting those in the region. Distributive benefits are usually distributed in the process of developing authorization and appropriations bills as part of the budgeting process.

Distributing policy allows for a considerable amount of negotiation and sharing of benefits among members of the National Assembly, because they cite their effectiveness in bringing money to their district in their effectiveness during reelection campaigns. In the United States, spending which benefits a particular district is called *pork-barrel spending*. There is a powerful incentive to engage in what political scientists call *logrolling,* in which members pledge to support each other's pork-barrel spending. For example, infrastructure investment is usually spread across many legislative districts in part to guarantee support for bills authorizing spending.

Distributive policy making is made even easier by the inability, in this style of policy making, to easily identify particular groups of people that are benefiting from the policy, while the costs of the policy are more broadly spread across society. Local officials and local assembly members depict these policies as good for the local community, but as being paid for by the entire nation through general funds. Indeed, local spending programs are often justified as a way of gaining a community's "fair share" of taxes paid by the district or city's taxpayers. Because of the actual or assumed benefits to particular people without any counter-balancing groups seeking to stop spending, there is little conflict over distributive policy. It is usually made fairly quickly, easily, and with a minimum amount of scrutiny given to individual spending decisions. When the news media or legislators do scrutinize such spending, there may be a call for reform of the system, but the benefits are so clear that the system of distributive policy endures.

Regulatory Policies

Regulatory policies are policies that are intended to govern the conduct of business. There are two broad types of regulatory policies.

Competitive regulatory policy involves policies designed to limit the provision of goods and services to specific providers chosen from a larger pool of competitors. Ripley and Franklin (1991) cite the allocation of radio and television frequencies and the awarding of cable television franchises as examples in the United States. Another example is regulation of trades or professions, such as setting licensing standards for lawyers, doctors, engineers, and other professions. This system assures professional oversight over the activities of professionals who must be trained and regulated to assure competent service to their clients. These policies, on the other hand, also create barriers to entering a profession, thereby limiting the number of professionals who provide a service and helping to keep costs high where the number of professionals is lower than it would otherwise be.

For the most part, competitive regulatory policy is made without much public scrutiny, attracting the attention of related business and professional groups, but much of this type of policy is relatively arcane and simulates little public notice.

Protective regulatory policy, on the other hand, is intended to protect the public at large from the negative effects of private activities, such as tainted food, air pollution, unsafe consumer products, or fraudulent business transactions. While most businesses and their leaders are responsible citizens who do not wish to hurt or alienate their customers, business are also motivated by profit. Businesses often resist regulation on cost grounds, saying that it would reduce or eliminate profit margins, make products uncompetitive in the market, and place firms at competitive disadvantage vis-à-vis less-regulated foreign competitors.

Redistributive Policy

Redistributive policy is controversial, involving policy making characterized by a high level of conflict and difficulty in changing policy once established. Redistributive policy is characterized by actions "intended to manipulate the allocation of wealth, property, personal or civil rights, or some other valued item among social classes or racial groups" (Ripley and Franklin, 1991).

Based on this definition, obvious examples include welfare, civil rights for social minorities (like the disabled), and aid to poor and less-developed areas. While there has been considerable redistributive policy making, these policies are difficult to pass because passage requires that the less powerful prevail over more powerful interests or at least persuade more powerful groups that it is right and just to approve the redistribution of some resource to the less powerful. This is illustrated by the difficulty in expanding broad social welfare benefits in Korea in spite of the creation of a welfare state as a regular item on the issue agenda across several elections.

Ripley and Franklin (1991) updated the typologies by dividing regulatory policy into two categories, protective regulation and competitive regulation (see Table 5-2).

[Table 5-2] Influence of Policy Types

Policy Type	Executive and centralized bureaucracy	Bureaus	Legislature	Legislature sub-committees	Private sector
Distributive	Low	High	Low (except sub-committees)	High	High (subsidized groups)
Protective regulatory	Moderately high	Moderate	Moderately high	Moderate	Moderately high (regulated interests)
Competitive regulatory	Low	High (regulatory agencies)	Low	Moderate to low	High (regulated interests)
Redistributive	High	High	High	Moderately low	High (clusters of interest groups)

Discussion Questions:

1. What are the strengths and weaknesses of the various policy instruments?

2. What are the factors that determine the choice of a policy instrument?

3. What is the advantage of dividing policies into Lowi's

typologies instead of dividing them into policy domains?

4. What are the differences between Lowi's typologies and those of Ripley and Franklin?

5. Why are distributive policies very popular?

6. Which political orientation (liberal or conservative) more often supports redistributive politics? Why do they take those stands?

Vocabulary

regulation
government management
taxing and spending
market mechanisms
exhortation
hortatory appeal
capacity building tool
policy typologies
distributive policy
redistributive policy
regulatory policy
pork-barrel spending
logrolling
protective regulation
competitive regulation

References

Birkland, Thomas A. 2001. *An Introduction to the Policy Process: Theories, Concepts, and Models of Public Policy Making.* New York: M. E. Sharpe.

Kraft, Michael E. and Furlong, Scott R. 2004. *Public Policy: Politics, Analysis, and Alternatives.* Washington, D.C.: CQ Press.

Lowi, Theodore J. 1964. "American Business, Public Policy, Case Studies, and Political Theory." *World Politics,* 16 (July): 667-715.

Lowi, Theodore J. 1979. *The End of Liberalism: The Second Republic of the United States.* 2nd ed. New York: W.W. Norton.

Ripley, Randall, and Franklin, Grace. 1991. *Congress, the Bureaucracy and Public Policy.* 5th ed. Pacific Grove, California: Brooks-Cole.

Steinberger, Peter J. 1980. "Typologies of Public Policy: Meaning Construction and the Policy Process." *Social Science Quarterly,* 61 (September): 185-197.

Stillman, Richard J. 1996. *The American Bureaucracy.* Chicago: Nelson-Hall.

WEEK 6 Public Policy Design and Policy Tools

Summary

The elements of policy design include the goals of policy, the causal model, the tools of policy, the targets of policy, and the implementation of the policy.

Policy tools are elements in policy design that cause agents or targets to do something hopefully in advance of the policy. Policy tools may use authority, inducements or sanctions, capacity-building, persuasion, and education. Policy tools are selected for political feasibility, availability of resources, and on the basis of behavioral assumptions.

13 Elements of Policy Design

Policy design refers to the careful consideration during policy formulation of the role of government "agents" and the "target population" – those who receive benefits or who are the objects of government regulation. Public policies must be thoroughly grounded in an understanding of the attitudes and motivations of the policy actors who will decide how the policies are implemented. This determines whether they succeed and whether they have the desired effects.

Decision makers must explicitly consider five elements of policy design, as listed in Table 6-1.

[Table 6-1] Elements of Policy Design

Element	Questions to ask
Policy Goals	What are the goals of the policy? To eliminate a problem? To alleviate a problem but not entirely eliminate it? To keep a problem from getting worse?
Causal Model	What is the casual model? Do you know that the result will be Y if we do X? How do we know this? If we do not know, how can we find out?
Policy Tools	What tools or instruments will be used to put the policy into effect? Will they be more or less coercive? Will they rely on incentives, persuasion, or information? Capacity building?
Policy Targets	Whose behavior is supposed to change? Are there direct and indirect targets? Are design choices predicated on our social construction of the target population?
Implementation	How will the program be implemented? Who will lay out the implementation system? Will a top down or bottom up design be selected? Why?

14 Policy Tools

Policy tools are elements in policy design that cause agents or targets to do something they would not do otherwise or modify behavior to solve public problems or attain policy goals.

The choice of such tools reflects different views of how people behave and what might lead them to change their behavior. Policy instruments or tools are means of control that are designed to cause people to do things, refrain from doing things, or continue doing things that they would otherwise not do.

15 Types of Policy Tools or Instruments

Schneider and Ingram (1993) distinguish five kinds of policy tools:

- Authority tools
- Inducements and sanctions
- Capacity-building tools
- Hortatory tools
- Learning tools

Authority Tools

These are pronouncements of policy that carry the force of law. They compel particular behaviors and compliance. People do things because someone in authority asks them to do so. The use such of tools, not always effective or democratic, depends on the perceived legitimacy of government. These tools may be particularly suitable during times of crisis when favorable responses by the public are more likely. Examples include criminal law and environmental regulations. Authority tools are also known as law (Peters, 1999), law and regulation (Levine et al., 1990), and directive power (Anderson, 2000).

Inducements and Sanctions

These are tools that induce voluntary or coerced actions based on tangible payoffs. The assumption is here that people are rational actors who seek to maximize their self interest. Inducements encourage people to act in a certain way because they will gain from doing so. Sanctions are negative incentives or penalties that are thought to discourage behavior that is inconsistent with policy goals. Examples include fines for violating regulations and bonus payments for timely completion of contracts.

Capacity-Building Tools

These tools involve training, technical assistance, education, and information needed for taking policy actions and empowering other agencies. They provide training, education, information, and technical assistance, and they aim to inform or enlighten and thus empower people, either those in the target population or policy agents. Examples include training, technology transfer, the provision of information to local government as well as cash transfers to hire more staff.

Hortatory Tools

These are attempts to persuade people to engage in desirable behaviors or to avoid engaging in undesirable behaviors. Governments invoke images and values through speeches, proclamations, and other communication to exhort people to behave in a certain way. Examples include public campaigns to change the birth rate, encourage voting, and discourage smoking. Hortatory tools are also known as suasion (Peters, 1999).

[Figure 6-1] Politicians Use Hortatory Tools

Learning Tools

These are tools to help understand the relevant aspects of policy problems. Policy agents and target populations are encouraged to participate and learn, for example, through citizen advisory panels and collaborative processes. Examples include focus groups, opinion polls, censuses, basic and applied research.

Other Tools

There are many different terms that can be used to categorize policy tools and other scholars have identified additional tools:

- Services
- Monetary tools
- Taxes
- Loans
- Contracting out
- Intergovernment grants
- General expenditures
- Property operation

- Subsidies
- Insurance
- Inspection
- Licensing
- Informal procedures

Services, also known as direct provision of goods or services (Levine et al., 1990), may be provided directly by government to users, including postal service, and weather forecasting.

Monetary tools, known as money (Peters, 1999) or transfer payments (Levine et al., 1990), involve the transfer of money to various interests, including retirement pensions, food assistance for the poor, and veterans' benefits.

Taxes as a policy tool cover policies intended to alter behavior by making some activities more or less economically desirable. Tax deductions for insurance or education or cash expenditures and free enterprise (or economic) zones are examples.

Loans, known also as loan and loan guarantees (Levine et al., 1990) or as other economic instruments (Peters, 1999), are government loans to induce economic activity or other desirable activity. The various subsidized education loans in the US are good examples of government loans.

Contracts and contracting out are where government entities contract with private firms to provide goods or services. Contracts to run bus lines as well as contracts to supply complex goods to government, such as military equipment, computers, or mass transit vehicles.

Intergovernmental grants are where different levels of government provide financial assistance, particularly where such money is given to help with particular programs. This may be a significant proportion of budgets for lower levels of government.

General expenditures represents general spending done by the government every day on the people, goods, and services it needs to function. This includes personnel costs, supplies, utilities, etc. (such spending has substantial national and local economic effects).

Market and property operation cover government activities that have private counterparts and that have economic and policy consequences. Examples include public corporations as well as the market activities of the Bank of Korea.

Subsidies are payments to ensure the economic viability of an activity, particularly when that activity addresses some broader goals. Examples include agricultural subsidies, various business subsidies, and subsidies to the film industry.

Insurance is provision of insurance where it is not generally available in the private insurance market or where government can more efficiently manage a more comprehensive insurance pool. National health insurance is a good example.

Inspection is where government conducts inspections to verify compliance with regulation. Examples may include safety audits or public accomodations, health inspections for restaurants, and audits and inspections of educational institutions.

Licensing is where a government authority provides permission to engage in an activity that is prohibited without such a license. Driver's licenses, professional licensing for physicians, lawyers, and engineers as well as licensing for hospitals, building permits, and corporate charters.

Informal procedures are practices not specified in law or regulation to resolve problems. A good example are negotiations with regulators for resolving disputes.

[Table 6-2] Types of Policy Tools or Instruments

Levine, Peters, and Thompson (1990)	Schneider and Ingram (1993)	Peters (1999)	Anderson (2000)
Law and regulation	Authority tools	Law	Directive power
Direct provision of goods or services		Services	Services
Transfer payments		Money	Benefits
Intergovernmental grants			
Contracting out			Contracts General expenditures
			Market and property operations
Tax system (tax expenditures)		Taxes	Taxes
Loan and loan guarantees		Other economic instruments	Loans
			Subsidies
Insurance			
	Hortatory tools	Suasion	
	Inducements and sanctions		Sanctions
	Capacity building tools		
	Learning tools		
			Inspection
			Licensing
			Informal procedures

16 Elements for Selecting Policy Tools

Policy designers must consider a number of elements in order to select a policy tool. Some of these are:

- Political feasibility
- Availability of resources
- Behavioral assumptions

Political Feasibility

Policy making is at least as much a political process as it is a technical process. Even technically superior policy tools may not be adopted because they are politically unpopular. For example, the United States has no equivalent of Korean National Health Insurance. Americans must get private health insurance, receive assistance from a public program, or go without, even though this leads to much higher costs than in systems with national health insurance or national healthcare.

In the face of a major youth unemployment problem, the government could directly provide a large number of jobs, but this solution would require a major expansion in the size of government and big tax increases. There is strong enough resistance to both that creating enough government jobs to solve the youth unemployment issue is not raised as a serious option.

Availability of Resources

A second factor in policy tool choice is the availability of resources for implementing policy. For example, there may be two ways to battle the problem of forest fires: posting thousands of lookouts in forests or employing a public education program to tell people that "only you can prevent forest fires," making a bear cub the symbol of that campaign. The US Forest Service chose the latter hortatory tool because it is much less expensive than more aggressive efforts to detect and prevent fires caused by carelessness.

[Figure 6-2] The US Has No National Health Insurance

As another example, Korea could use hortatory tools to discourage littering, but it does not have strict enforcement of anti-littering laws because there are many people available to pick up litter off the streets at a low labor cost.

Behavioral Assumptions

The final element for selecting policy tools depends on the policy theory. That is, what causes the problem and how can a particular policy change people's behavior to produce the desired result? For example, monetary policy is based on behavioral assumptions about the market. One assumption is that a lower exchange rate with the US dollar will increase exports. Another assumption is that increased exports would increase employment and other desired outcomes.

Discussion Questions:

1. What are the elements of policy design?
2. What are policy tools?
3. What are the different kinds of tools?
4. How are policy tools selected?

Vocabulary

policy goals
causal model
policy tools
policy targets
policy implementation
authority tools
inducements and sanctions
capacity-building tools
hortatory tools
learning tools
political feasibility
availability of resources
behavioral assumptions

References

Affholter, Dennis P. 1994. "Outcome Monitoring." In *Handbook of Practical Program Evaluation.* Ed. Joseph S. Wholey, Harry P. Harty, and Kathryn E. Newcomer. San Francisco: Josse Bass.

Anderson, James E. 2000. *Public Policymaking.* 4th ed. Boston: Houghton Mifflin.

Birkland, Thomas A. 2001. *An Introduction to the Policy Process: Theories, Concepts, and Models of Public Policy Making.* New York: M. E. Sharpe.

Ingram, Helen and Mann, Dean. 1980. "Policy Failure: An Issue Deserving Attention." In *Why Policies Succeed or Fail.* Ed. Helen Ingram and Dean Mann. Beverly Hills: Sage.

Kraft, Michael E. and Furlong, Scott R. 2004. *Public Policy: Politics, Analysis, and Alternatives.* Washington, D.C. CQ Press.

Laumann, Edward O., and Knoke, David. 1987. *The Organizational State: Social Choice in National Policy Domains.* Madison: University of Wisconsin Press.

Levine, Charles H., Peters, B. Guy, and Thompson, Frank J. 1990. *Public Administration: Challenges, Choices, Consequences.* Glenview, Illinois: Scott, Foresman/Little Brown.

Peters, B. Guy. 1999. *American Public Policy: Promise and Performance.* Chappaqua, New York: Chatham House/Seven Rivers.

Schneider, Anne and Ingram, Helen. 1993. "The Social Construction of Target Populations: Implications for Politics and Policy." *American Political Science Review,* 87 (22): 334-348.

Stone, Deborah. 1997. *Policy Paradox: The Art of Political Decision Making.* New York: W.W. Norton.

WEEK 7 Analyzing Public Policy

Summary

Policy analysis is a systematic way of evaluating public policy alternatives as well as existing government programs. It is especially important in policy formulation. The nature of policy analysis is that it refers to the assessment of policy alternatives.

The types of analysis include scientific, professional, and political.

The steps in policy analysis are defining and analyzing the problem, constructing alternatives, developing evaluative criteria, assessing the alternatives, and drawing conclusions.

17 Definition and Nature of Policy Analysis

Policy analysis is usually described as a systematic and organized way of evaluating public policy alternatives or existing government programs. It often involves applying economic tools and other quantitative methods or measures. Policy analysis may therefore seem to some students of public policy to hold little relevance to anyone except policy specialists, but in reality everyone uses policy analysis in many day-to-day activities. Buying a car, selecting a particular college course, or choosing a restaurant for dinner all require thinking about the pluses and minuses of the available choices. This includes any decision about how to spend money.

[Figure 7-1] Choosing a Restaurant for Dinner Requires Thinking about Choices

Policy analysis can be used throughout the policy process, but it becomes especially important in the formulation of policies and evaluation of programs after they are implemented. In assessing a public problem, policy analysis may assist in describing its scope, such as the percentage of people in poverty. When developing alternatives and choosing a direction, a decision maker can use analysis to assess the feasibility of the choices based on economic, administrative, political, and ethical criteria. The same methods can be used to evaluate a program to determine its effectiveness, or whether it has achieved its expected results.

What is Policy Analysis?

Analysis means deconstructing an object of study. That means breaking it down into its basic elements to understand it better. Policy analysis is the examination of components of public policy, the policy process, or both. In another way, it is the study of the causes and consequences of policy decisions. MacRae and Wilde (1979) called policy analysis the use of reason and evidence to choose the best policy among a number of alternatives.

Policy analysis represents systematic thinking about public issues or decisions leading to practical responses that can be broadly communicated. The sponsor or producer of the work is not as important as the product, which is central. A policy must be considered for its system, practicality, and communications. All three of these dimensions are required for analysis.

Policy analysis uses many different methods of inquiry and draws from various disciplines to obtain the information needed to assess a problem and think clearly about alternative ways to resolve it. The same information also shapes public debate and deliberation over what actions to take. Policy analysis encourages deliberate critical thinking about the causes of public problems, the various approaches government and/or non-governmental actors might take, and which policy choices make the most sense.

Policy analysis may mean examining the components of the policy-making process, such as policy formulation and implementation, or substantive public policy issues, or both. The process usually involves collecting and interpreting information that clarifies the causes and effects of public problems and the likely consequences of using one policy option or another to address them.

Analysis often means bringing scientific knowledge to the political process or "speaking truth to power." Policy analysis involves both descriptive (empirical) study, which tries to determine the facts of a given situation, and normative or value-based assessment of the options.

The Nature of Policy Analysis

Policy analysis most often refers to assessment of policy alternatives. It is the systematic investigation of alternative policy options and the assembly and integration of the evidence for and against each option. Policy analysis is not intended to make policy decisions but to inform the process of public debate and deliberation.

The study of public policy and the conduct of policy analysis are rarely simple matters. Public problems are usually complex and multifaceted, and people are bound to disagree intensely over how serious they are, what might be done about them, and the role of government in relation to the private sector. Some problems, such as global climate change or the challenge of international terrorism, are monumental. Some, such as how best to provide for a high quality public school system or limit urban sprawl, may be a bit easier to grasp. However, none are simple. If they were, the course of action would be clear and not very controversial – removing snow and collecting trash, for example. Unfortunately, dealing with most problems is not so straightforward.

One of the primary functions of policy analysis is to satisfy the need for pertinent information and thoughtful and impartial assessments in the policy process. The information may not be widely available, or citizens and policy makers may not be able to understand it sufficiently, particularly when decisions must be made quickly because of impending deadlines or when the issues are politically controversial.

Under these conditions, policy analysis can clarify the issues, the available alternatives, and the effects of decisions that citizens and policy makers might choose to make. Policy analysis essentially involves looking ahead to anticipate the consequences of decisions and thinking seriously and critically about them. It is an alternative to "shooting from the hip" or making snap decisions based on ideology, personal experience, or limited or biased analysis of what should be done.

The solution to any controversial public problem is rarely achieved by relying solely on government agency officials, policy analysts, or other experts. The "best" solution will always be a matter of judgment and political choice because questions inevitably arise about the likely effectiveness of the policies chosen, their costs, who gains and who loses as a result, or whether the action can be justified on ethical or moral grounds. Policy analysis has been called an intellectual activity that takes place within a political setting. Its character and impact reflect that reality.

The politics are readily apparent in policy areas such as abortion rights, rights to privacy, or the use of public funds to support private school education where issues touch on basic questions of values. These kinds of policy choices reflect a combination of political preferences and an impartial assessment of the problem and possible solutions. In this context, policy analysis can pinpoint the nature of the problem, the policy choices available, and how each choice stands up against the different standards of judgment that might be used. People discuss government and public policy issues in many different settings: at home, in school, at work, and in bars and restaurants. In many cases the commentary is informal and can tend toward simplistic statement about, for instance, government proposals for some kind of policy change, from reducing crime rates to providing better health care services.

Citizens often air their views about government, politics, and public policy. Indeed, they hold strong opinions about what should be done about various problems. Even so, they may not think systematically about why the problems exist in the first place or what kind of policy action is most appropriate. Policy analysts hope to raise the level of such discussions, even if it remains unlikely that general conversations will be anchored in data analysis.

18 Types of Policy Analysis

The abundance of policy studies reflects not only the dramatic rise in the number of think tanks but also the increase in the number of interest groups that seek to shape opinion on the issues and affect policy process. Prominent think tanks, interest groups, and policy-oriented law firms and consulting companies tend to establish their offices in the capitol, or in the main city of a province, but organized interest groups are found all over most countries. Whether they are unions, environmental activists, corporate trade associations, or proessional organizations, they all have a stake in policy decisions made by government, and most set up a public or governmental affairs office to monitor pending legislation or agency acts.

Policy analysis organizations often continue to thrive in a country because of the character of government institutions and the political process. Fragmentation of government authority creates many opportunities for both interest group lobbying and policy analysis conducted outside of government. As political parties have weakened, interest group and think tank activity has increased.

The large number of think tanks and active interest groups almost guarantees that the public and policy makers will suffer from information overload as they try to make sense of the excess of reports and studies available on any public policy topic. Wilson (1998) observed that people are "drowning in information, while starving for wisdom." The future will belong to those capable of synthesizing information to make it usable.

This synthesizer is the policy analyst who is able to put together the right information at the right time, think critically about it, and make important choices wisely. Analysis, however, comes in many varieties, and policy makers and the public need to be able to differentiate the more worthy from the less worthy.

Policy analysis falls into three broad categories: scientific, professional, and political. All serve valid purposes but have varying goals and objectives and use different methods. Table 7-1 offers a summary of the distinctions among the three perspectives.

[Table 7-1] Types of Policy Analysis

Type of analysis	Objectives	Approaches	Limitations	Examples
Scientific	Search for "truth" and build theory about policy actions and effects	Use the scientific method to test hypotheses and theories; aim for objective and rigorous analysis; policy relevance less important than advancing knowledge	May be too theoretical and not adequately address information needs of decision makers	Academics and natural scientists, National Academy of Sciences, Intergovernmental Panel on Climate Change
Professional	Analyze policy alternatives for solving public problems	Synthesize research and theory to understand consequences of policy alternatives; evaluate current programs and their effects; aim for objectivity, but with goal of practical in policy debate	Research and analysis may be too narrow due to time and resource constraints; may neglect fundamental causes of public problems	Korea Institute for International Economic Policy, Korea Institute for Public Administration, National Assembly Budget Office

Political	Advocate and support preferred policies	Use legal, economic, and political arguments consistent with value positions; level of objectivity and rigor varies; aim to influence policy debate to realize organizational goals and values	Often ideological or partisan and may not be credible; may lack analytic depth	New Frontier Party, New Politics Alliance for Democracy, FKTU, KLUC, KCTU

For example, social science studies in the scientific category are not typically intended to influence public policy directly. Their purpose is to deepen, broaden, and extend policy makers' capacity for judgment, not to provide them with answers. In contrast, work that falls into the professional category, such as policy analysis from think tanks, is nearly always directed at policy makers with the clear intent of providing answers to policy questions.

Some think tanks should be placed in the political category because they have explicit ideological missions. All think tanks conduct analysis and advocate positions on public policy issues, but some of these groups are committed to political or ideological positions that affect their analyses and recommendations.

[Table 7-2] Policy Analysis Steps

Steps	Types of Questions	Illustrations
Define and analyze the problem	What is the problem faced? Where does it exist? Who or what is affected? How did it developed? What are the major causes? How might the causes be affected by policy action?	How is cell phone use related to auto accidents? What is the potential to reduce accident rates through policy action? How does cell phone use compare to other distractions while driving?
Construct policy alternatives	What policy options might be considered for dealing with the problem?	Should governments institute fines to reduce cell phone use while driving? Should government try to educate drivers on cell phone use? Is it technologically feasible to disable cell phones in a moving car?
Develop evaluative criteria	What criteria are most suitable for the problem and the alternatives? What are the costs of action? What is the likely effectiveness? Social and political feasibility? Equity?	What criteria are most important for regulation of cell phones? What options might be most effective in discouraging drivers from using phones? Will people find these options acceptable? Is it ethical to restrict individual behavior to achieve a social goal?
Assess the alternatives	Which alternatives are better than others? What kind of analysis might help to distinguish better and worse policy alternatives? Is the evidence available? If not, how can it be produced?	Are fines or education more likely to reduce drivers' cell phone use? How successful are the efforts of government to regulate cell phone use? What evidence is needed to answer these questions?
Draw Conclusions	Which policy option is the most desirable given the circumstances and the evaluative criteria? What other factors should be considered?	Should government impose stiff fines? Would fines be accepted as a legitimate action? How might the action be made more acceptable?

19 Steps in the Policy Analysis Process

The word analysis comes from the Greek word meaning to break down into component parts. Teachers of policy analysis usually specify the components of the analytical process as a series of steps. The most common approach to policy analysis is to picture it as a series of analytical steps or stages, which are the elements of rational problem solving. According to models of rational decision making, you define a problem, indicate the goals and objectives to be sought, consider a range of alternative solutions, evaluates each of the alternatives to clarify their consequences, and then recommend or choose the alternative with the greatest potential for solving the problem. This process is similar to the way most people make everyday decisions, although they do it much more casually.

Table 7-2 summarizes the major steps of policy analysis and the kinds of questions analysts pose. It also illustrates how each stage of analysis might apply to a particular policy problem. Each step is considered briefly here as a description of what policy analysis aspires to do.

Define and Analyze the Problem

Defining the problem is the first step of policy analysis. Problem is different as a general term and an analytical term. For policy analysts the term specifically refers to the existence of an unsatisfactory set of conditions for which relief is sought, either through private means or by government. Analysts therefore need to describe that set of conditions, usually through the collection of pertinent facts or data on its magnitude or extent. For example, who is affected by it and how seriously? How long has the situation existed and how might it change over the next several years or decades? How amenable is it to intervention through one means or another? The goals and objectives of such intervention, whether private or governmental, may not be clear to all concerned.

It may also be necessary to clarify what is the meant by the set of conditions, to define it clearly, and to develop accurate measures of it. If the problem is youth unemployment in Korea, for example, an analyst would need to be clear about what is meant by youth unemployment, how to determine the extent of it, and who is affected by it. A great deal of information has been gathered on this problem: the Ministry of Labor reported in 2006 that 10% of youth aged 15~29 were unemployed and this had increased to 11.1% by 2015. However, "unemployment" means participating actively in the labor force but without a job. This means that most of the young people without jobs are not considered unemployed because they are studying for an employment test or preparing for work but not currently actively applying for a job. During this same period, the employment percentage gives a clearer view of the youth employment problem. Only 40.5% of youth aged 15~29 held a job in 2009, 40.3% in 2010, 40.5% in 2011, 40.4% in 2012, and 39.7% in 2013 (MOEL, 2015). Clearly, choosing a different measure frames the problem very differently. Looking at unemployment statistics makes it look like a problem of one in ten, whereas looking at employment statistics makes the problem appear to be much more urgent, affecting about six out of ten Korean youth. Analysts will want to develop quantitative measures of this kind for most public problems.

Beyond gathering basic information about the problem, analysts want to identify its causes, which is not always an easy task. Without a good idea of how and why the problem came about, however, it is difficult to think usefully about possible solutions. This kind of diagnosis of the problem is similar to what a physician does when a patient is ill or what a mechanic does when a car is not operating.

The importance of the diagnosis is clear when looking at how policy makers try to cope with an issue as large as global terrorism. Policy actions are unlikely to be effective without understanding the causes of terrorism, even though they may be too numerous to address easily. As a more concrete example, an analyst must explain why safety precautions are not followed in public accomodations before seeking a solution. Otherwise, there is little reason to believe that specific actions will improve the quality of schools.

Construct Policy Alternatives

Constructing policy alternatives is perhaps the most important stage in the policy analysis process. If analysts and policy makers cannot think of creative ways of solving problems, conventional approaches that may no longer be appropriate will continue. Early in the process, therefore, analysts are called upon to think imaginatively and critically about how the problem might be addressed, both within government and outside of it.

One approach that has gained increasing acceptance is privatization, the transfer of public services from government to the private sector. Such private sector solutions, recommended by many policy analysts and organizations, and sometimes endorsed by government, are said to be more appealing, and perhaps more effective, than reliance on a government agency. Many public services are turned over to private companies for management. For example, there are private companies that run bus service, there are both private and public schools and universities, there are private security companies, and there are even private jails in the United States.

[Figure 7-2] Private Bus Service is a Policy Alternative

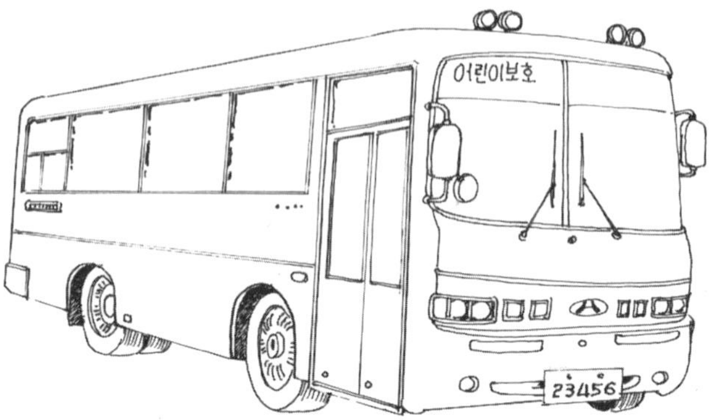

Choose the Evaluative Criteria

When policy alternatives have been identified, the analysis shifts to assessing their potential. This task calls for selecting suitable evaluation criteria. There are other appropriate criteria, such as ethics, feasibility (political, administrative, technical), environmental impact, and any number of political values, such as personal freedom, against which to assess policy proposals. No matter how long a list of potential evaluative criteria analysis might develop, some criteria will be more appropriate for a given problem than others.

For example, the Park Administration conducted a defense review to determine the most effective way to counter the nuclear and missile threat posed by North Korea's advanced weapons systems it has promised to use against South Korea.

The analysis concluded that the Terminal High Altitude Area Defense (THAAD) system developed by the United States would be the most effective way to counter North Korean weapons technology. On what basis should analysts evaluate the proposal, particularly in relation to other national security issues? One criterion would have to be the effect on other security relationships. Because of the range of the radar system, the Chinese and Russians have criticized Korean deployment of the system as it could monitor them as well as North Koreans. What about the costs? The system would cost $1.82 billion, amounting to more than two trillion won. Who would pay the costs? Is this outlay of money reasonable in light of the gains to the nation's defense and the risk that the Chinese and Russians might be offended? How would an analysis go about determining the answer?

Plenty of information is available about the missile defense system, but a good deal of it is contradictory, and analysts disagree so any assessment of the desirability of creating and funding a system as technically complex as the THAAD missile defense is a demanding undertaking. Nevertheless, policy makers and analysts need to ask the questions and try to find answers. Because multiple criteria for evaluating such proposals exist, students of public policy need to be aware of them and be prepared to think about which criteria are best suited to making the correct choices for society.

For some policy actions, for example, whether and how to engage with North Korea, the evaluative criteria would likely include political values. National security will be weighed against other needs, such as family reunions and the desire for national reunification. As this example indicates, conflicts may arise between criteria. On what basis should policy analysts, citizens, and policy makers judge the suitability of policy options? How is it possible to reconcile the short-term national security implications of preventing North Korean attack versus the longer-term need to deal with the root causes of national division?

Assess the Alternatives

Analysts ask in this stage which of the several alternatives that might be considered seriously is most likely to produce the outcome sought, whether that outcome is to reduce the crime rate, improve the plight of the homeless, raise educational quality, protect the environment, or whatever. This exercise involves making judgments about how well each policy option fits in relation to the most relevant criteria. Analysts might rank the options in terms of overall desirability or consider the options in terms of each criterion, such as effectiveness, cost, and equity.

Some specialists refer to this stage of the process as projecting the outcomes or assessing impacts. A number of different methods or tools are used to do this such as cost-benefit analysis, cost-effectiveness, risk assessment, decision analysis, forecasting, impact assessment, and ethical analysis.

Analysts have many ways to present the alternatives so that policy makers and other interested parties can understand the analysis and the choices they face. For example, if three policy options are offered for consideration, the analyst might present each in terms of its likely effectiveness, economic efficiency, and equity. Tradeoffs are inevitable in this kind of decision making. Only rarely does a given policy option rank highest on all of the evaluative criteria. It is far more likely that one option is judged to be most effective, but another cheaper or more equitable in its effects. Analysts, therefore, attach weight to each criterion.

For example, is equity more important than efficiency in promoting the cleanup of hazardous waste sites? Should government clean up the most dangerous sites first or try to ameliorate the conditions at several sites at once? Or should the resources be directed to sites that have a disproportionate impact on poor and minority communities? Would doing so promote greater equity? As analysts consider more than a few conflicting bases for assessing policy options, the necessity for weighting criteria increases.

Draw Conclusions

Analysts summarize their findings and draw conclusions about the relative merits of competing policy proposals, but leave the choice of policy action to policy makers and the public. Whichever approach is taken, one must bear in mind that all analysis is necessarily partial and limited. That is, analysis can never be complete in the sense of covering every conceivable question that might be raised. It cannot be free of limitations, either, because every method or tool that might be used is subject to some constraints. Policy analysts need to develop a robust ability to deal with uncertainty, which comes with the process.

It may sometimes be difficult to draw a conclusion. In that case, students of policy analysis are advised to learn to ask critical questions about the information they collect, especially regarding its validity.

Where did the information come from, and how reliable is the source?

Is there any way to double-check the facts and their

interpretation? Does the information and analysis seem believable?

Are there any signs of bias that might affect the conclusions that the study offers?

If two or more studies contradict one another, what are the reasons?

Is it because of political ideologies, differences in the preferred policy actions, or differences in the way the problem is defined?

Are the authors too selective in deciding what information should be presented and what can be left out?

By gathering information from multiple sources and comparing different interpretations, students might find it easier to determine which of the studies is the most credible.

Discussion Questions:

1. What is policy analysis? What does it mean to bring scientific knowledge to the political process?

2. What is the nature of policy analysis?

3. How can policy alternatives be assessed?

4. What are the different types of analysis?

5. What are the steps of policy analysis?

Vocabulary

policy goals
causal model
policy tools
policy targets
policy implementation
authority tools

inducements and sanctions
capacity-building tools
hortatory tools
learning tools
political feasibility
availability of resources
behavioral assumptions

References

Birkland, Thomas A. 2001. *An Introduction to the Policy Process: Theories, Concepts, and Models of Public Policy Making.* New York: M. E. Sharpe.

Dunn, N. William. 1981. *An Introduction Public Policy Analysis.* Englewood Cliffs, New Jersey: Prentice-Hall, Inc.

Kingdon, John W. 1995. *Agendas, Alternatives and Public Policies.* 2nd ed. New York: Harper Collins.

Kraft, Michael E. and Furlong, Scott R. 2004. *Public Policy: Politics, Analysis, and Alternatives.* Washington, D.C. CQ Press.

MacRae, Duncan, and Wilde, James. 1979. *Policy Analysis for Public Decisions.* North Scituate, Massachusetts: Duxbury.

Ministry of Employment and Labor. 2015. "Major Statistics," August 10, 2015, from http://www.moel.go.kr/english/pas/pasMajor.jsp

Randall R. Bovbjerg. 1985. What Is Policy Analysis? *Journal of Policy Analysis and Management*, 5(1), Autumn: 154-158.

Shin, Yong-Ho, Jeong, Yong-Soo, and Ser, Myo-Ja. 2015 "Gov't Concludes THAAD is Best Option for Korea." *Korea JoongAng Daily*, May 21, 2015 from http://koreajoongangdaily.joins.com/news/article/Article.aspx?aid=3004458

Stokey, Edith and Zeckhauser, Richard. 1978. *A Primer for Policy Analysis.* New York: W.W. Norton & Company.

Weimer, L. David, and Vining, R. Aidan. 2005. *Policy Analysis: Concepts and Practice*. Pearson, New Jersey: Prentice Hall.

Wilson, Edward O. 1998. *Consilience: The Unity of Knowledge.* New York: Knopf.

"Youth Unemployment in Korea on the Rise." *English Chosun*, December 24, 2007, from http://english.chosun.com/w21data/html/news/200712/200712240012.html

WEEK 8 The Public Policy Process

Summary

Any problem definition represents one of many possible points of view. Defining a problem is not enough. Agenda setting is the process of bringing problems to the attention of elites and the public. Items on the agenda need to travel from systematic attention to the institutional agenda to the decision agenda before they are acted upon.

Policy formulation may be routine, analogous, or creative and involves both formal and informal actors.

Policy legitimation is an essential process for any political system as politics is based on legitimacy. It is both a simple and complex process at the same time and involves both formal and informal actors in a dynamic process.

Implementation is the process of putting a policy into effect. Implementation involves interpretation, organization, and application. The techniques for effecting implementation include early planning, scheduling models, expediters, incentives, participation, the case management system, and management by objectives. Implementation may be affected by internal and external factors and may be based on a top-down, bottom-up, or synthesis approach.

Evaluation is the measurement of the desirable and undesirable consequences of policies. The process consists of identifying the goals, putting the goal activity into operation, assessing the effect, value formation, goal-setting, and goal measuring. Evaluation involves assumptions about values and objectives. The functions of evaluation include information, revealing goals, clarifying values, creating alternative policy sources, and contributing to the application of other policy analyses. It may be done through experimentation, network analysis, PERT, or the critical path method. It may be based on economic or professional models.

Policy termination is the final step in the policy process, but should not be the last step in terms of consideration. It includes functions, organizations, policies, and programs and is relatively rare.

20 Defining Problems and Agenda Setting

Figure 8-1 draws an overall picture of the policy process. Problem definition is a matter of representation because every description of a situation is a portrayal from only one of many points of view. Problem definition is strategic because groups, individuals, and government agencies deliberately and consciously fashion portrayals so as to promote their favored course of action. An individual's perspective and background determine how they define a problem and relate to it. Personal ideology and values are likely to influence how a problem is defined or even if the individual considers a situation to be

[Figure 8-1] The Policy Process

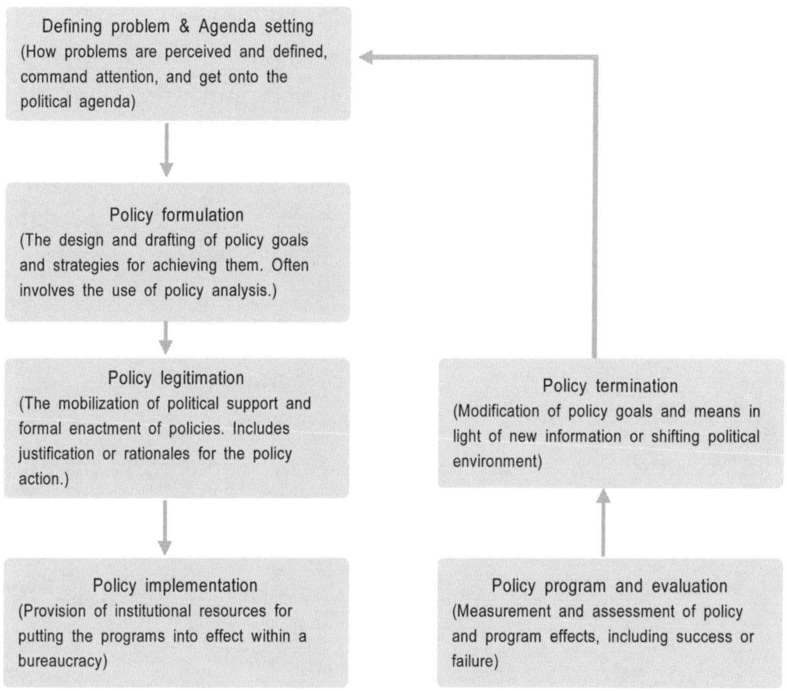

a problem at all.

For example, the issue of Internet pornography could be defined as one of public morality and child protection, as it usually is in Korea. Alternately, it could be defined in terms of free expression, as it often is in the United States, with very different implications. Family planning might be thought of as a simple public health issue, or it may be defined in moral and ethical terms and associated with abortion, or seen as a matter of women's rights and privacy. Making comparisons is part of problem definition.

By supplying new and often objective information on the nature of a problem and its implications, policy analysts can help to steer political debate toward a rational assessment of the scope of the problem, its causes, and possible solutions. For example, a study of urban sprawl might highlight adverse impacts on highway congestion, land use, and water supplies and suggest how better growth management could minimize those effects. The findings and recommendations of such a study would no doubt differ significantly from the arguments of real estate developers and pro-growth public officials.

Defining problems is not enough to find solutions, or formulate policy. A problem must rise high enough on the agenda. It is not easy for societal problems to reach agenda status because so many problems are competing for social and political attention at any particular time. Some make it onto the agenda and some do not. The agenda is a collection of problems, understandings of causes, symbols, solutions, and other elements of the public and government officials. An agenda can be as a concrete list of bills that are before a legislature, but also includes a series of beliefs about the existence and magnitude of problems and how they should be addressed by government, the private sector, nonprofit organizations, or through joint action by some or all of these institutions.

Agenda setting is the process by which problems and alternative solutions gain or lose public and elite attention. An agenda is a collection of understandings, causes, symbols, solutions, and other elements of public problems that come to the attention of members of the public and government officials. Agenda setting is central to the policy process. If an issue does not attract appropriate attention, chances are it will languish without a government response. Therefore, the public policy student needs to understand what facilitates the movement of certain issues onto the agenda. Obviously, government elites can define a problem and raise its viability.

The agenda is actually quite vast. It is useful to think of several levels of the agenda, as shown in Figure 8-2. The broadest level of the agenda is the agenda universe, which contains all ideas that could possibly be brought up and discussed in a society or a political system.

The vast numbers of ideas in the agenda universe are more or less "acceptable" in a political sense, and have the potential to move to and appear on the systemic agenda.

[Figure 8-2] Levels of the Agenda

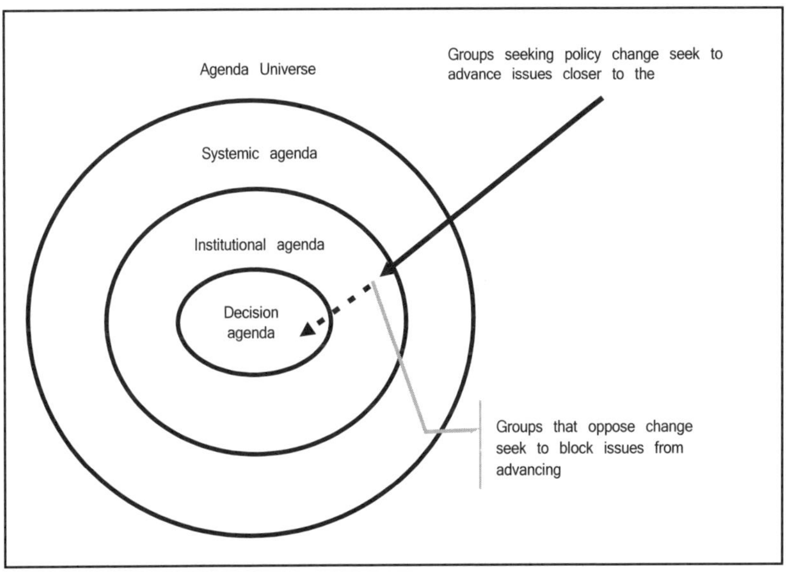

The systemic agenda consists of all issues that are commonly perceived by members of the political community as meriting public attention and as involving matters within the legitimate jurisdiction of existing government authority. The boundary between the systemic agenda and the agenda universe represents the current limit of the legitimate jurisdiction of existing government authority. That boundary can move in or out to accommodate more or fewer ideas over time. The institutional agenda is that list of items explicitly up for the active and serious consideration of authoritative decision makers. The limited amount of time or resources available to any institution or society means that only a limited number of issues is likely to reach the institutional agenda. The decision agenda contains items that are about to be acted upon by governmental body. Bills introduced and heard in a legislative committee are relatively low on the decision agenda until they are reported to the whole body for a vote.

Figure 8-2 implies that, except for the limitless agenda universe, the agenda and each level within it is finite and no society or political system can address all the possible alternatives to all possible problems that arise at any time. The agenda is finite so interests must compete with each other to get their issues and their preferred policy alternatives on the agenda. Some issues automatically make it to the agenda. They are mandated or required actions that government must address. The annual budget, legislation to reauthorize existing programs, and acting on presidential nominees for executive appointments automatically make it on to the agenda.

Policy makers would rather deal with a problem the public believes is important than with an issue that people are ignoring. The issue with the best chance of getting on the agenda would be one that is highly salient, but low in conflict, and issues with the worst chance would have low salience and high levels of conflict.

[Figure 8-3] The Government Addresses Issues on the Decision Agenda

21 Policy Formulation

Formulation is a derivative of "formula" and means simply developing a plan, a method, or a prescription for alleviating some need or for acting on a problem. It is the first stage of policy development. There is no set method for it to proceed. Policy formulation is the development of proposed courses of action to help resolve a public problem. Formulation is a technical as well as a political process. Policies that are carelessly formulated are more likely to fail, for example, through using inadequate data, questionable projections, or unreasonable assumptions.

Types of Formulation

There are many types of formulation based on the classification criteria. For example, there can be any number of categories by subject matter – formulation of courses of action for economic problems, education problems, military problems, and so on. Each has a different set of institutional units from which formulators are drawn. One of the most interesting and useful ways of classifying formulation is by the nature of decision making. Three types are offered here:

- Routine formulation
- Analogous formulation
- Creative formulation

Routine formulation means regularly reformulating similar proposals within an issue-area that has a well-established place on the government agenda.

Analogous formulation means treating a new problem by relying on what was done in developing proposals for similar problems in the past: searching for analogies.

Creative formulation means treating any problem with an essentially unprecedented proposal, one that represents a break with past practice.

Guidelines to Assist in Formulation Analysis:

- Formulation does not need to be limited to one set of actors. There may be two or more groups of formulators producing competing (or complementary) proposals.
- Formulation may proceed without the problem ever being very clearly defined, or without formulators ever having much contact with the effected groups.
- There is no necessary connection between formulation and particular institutions, thought it is a frequent activity of executive agencies.
- Formulation and reformulation may occur over a long

period of time without ever building sufficient support for any single proposal.
- There are often several points of appeal for those who lose at any level in the formulation process.
- The formulation process itself is never neutral.

Who is Involved in Policy Formulation?

It is not possible to list all actors involved in formulation across all issue areas. However, it is possible to identify the places to look for participation. Policy formulators can be categorized into two general groups (see Week 3):

- Formal policy actors (government)
- Informal policy actors (general public, interest groups)

Formal policy actors work in government such as legislators, chief executives, and agency officials, for example, who are especially influential in policy formulation. Appointed and career officials in a bureaucracy are among the most experienced and knowledgeable policy actors in most policy areas. They have the technical information needed to develop policy and the political knowledge that comes from working in the policy arena.

Interest groups, universities, professionals, and private research organizations are some of the informal policy actors. Each of them contributes substantially to formulating policy. Formal and informal policy actors correspond to official and unofficial actors.

The executive is typically seen as the source of planning. In Korea, the president and close associates in the Blue House and the cabinet establish the goals and establish the priorities that set the boundaries for formulation of proposals. The actual development of plans and proposals normally occurs within the bureaucracy, with formal clearance of actions by the upper echelons of political decision making. Legislators are also frequently involved in formulation. In fact, it is quite conceivable that a particular formulation network is drawn entirely from legislative actors, to include staff people, other legislative support units, and those groups outside government whose primary access is within the National Assembly.

Interest groups are active contributors to policy formulation. Like the bureaucracy, interest groups have a great deal of information at their disposal to provide background or specific solutions to problems. This information ranges from technical details about the problem to judgments about whether a proposal is likely to have political support.

Interest groups also attempt to shape policy to serve their own economic or political needs.

Cross-institutional and inter-level policy networks can be important, but it is still essential that institutional limits be acknowledged and assessed for their effect on policy formulation. Individual decision makers may communicate and otherwise interact with those outside their agency or committee. Even so, they are limited by certain features of the constitutional order and existing authority. The constitutional separation of powers and checks and balances establish a decision-making context that cannot be ignored in the study of public policy. The growth of peculiar policy relationships within agencies and committees that come to influence whether and how problems are defined and proposals developed. Incrementalism comes about in part because institutional characteristics limit what can be done. An agency accustomed to doing things a particular way will not innovate very often. Instead there is an effort to integrate new demands into an existing pattern of doing business.

[Figure 8-4] Agents of Policy Making and Avenues of Policy Formation

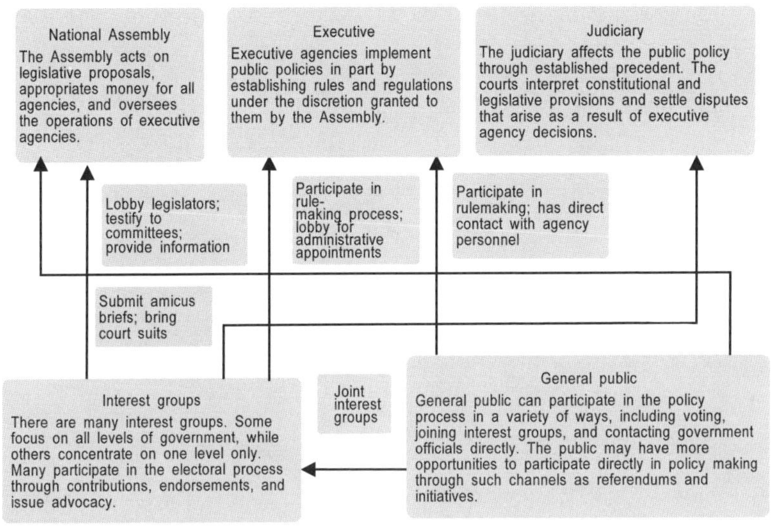

Policy makers are not faced with a single given problem at a time. Formulation is not institution-bound. It may result in one proposal or several and it may proceed with several clear definitions of the problem or no clear definition. It is also worth stressing that formulators make important linkages between problems and policies.

22 Policy Legitimation

Legitimacy is central to the existence of a political state.

It involves authority, consent, obligation, and support. Indeed, legitimacy involves the spectrum of government relationships with people and their problems. Some questions are mentioned for exploring the idea here. Why should anyone obey anyone else including governmental officials? Under what conditions should one obey and who says what those conditions are? Should anyone have the last word?

[Figure 8-5] Legitimacy : Why Should Anyone Obey Government Officials?

Legitimacy is based on attitudes that are learned. It is obviously essential for a political system, though legitimacy can be managed in society. Incongruity among public attitudes can cause complications as legitimacy may be in the eye of the beholder. Even so, legitimacy can be measured in a political system at any point in time.

Policy legitimation is defined as giving legal force to decisions or authorizing or justifying policy action. It may come from a majority vote in a legislature or a formal executive, bureaucrats, or judicial decision. The process of legitimation includes the legitimacy of the action taken, whether it is thought to be a proper exercise of government authority. This is a question of broad acceptability to the public and/or other policy actors.

Is Legitimation Simple or Complex?

Legitimation is both a simple and complex step in the policy process. It is simple when it merely means that a recognized authority considers and approves a policy proposal. A bill becomes a law at the national level when the National Assembly approves it and the president signs it. Legitimation may follow from a process of political instruction and debate that involves all major interests and a full and open airing of issues and controversies. Sometimes lawmakers call on actors, recording artists, athletes, and other celebrities to convince the public of the worthiness of an issue under consideration.

Process of Legitimation

Legitimation does not mean achievement of any particular measure of legitimacy. Officials must move ahead as though they knew what they are doing. The principle process of legitimation in a democracy is building a majority coalition. Majority rule is a cornerstone of democratic theory. It is a practical way of getting from political equality and popular sovereignty to a working government. While majority building is the principal process of legitimation, a number of sub processes also exist. For example, if an agency is authorized to establish standards, make contracts, grant resources, or make decisions of any other kind, it must develop legitimate processes by which choices are made.

An agency may, in fact, have the authority to create a complete policy process – defining the problem, formulating proposals, legitimating programs or standards etc. In many cases the choice of one alternative over another is made after consultation with affected groups or following public hearings similar to those conducted in a legislature. Legitimation is involved wherever methods have to be developed to authorize further action.

Who is Involved?

Legitimation is most closely identified in a democracy with the legislature. Therefore, legislators are surely involved, but majorities may also be put together through the efforts of bureaucrats, legislative staff, lobbyists, provincial and local officials, and the president.

Legitimation is dynamic attribute of any political system. This is particularly the case in democracies where the people presumably have the collective power to ascribe or withhold legitimacy. If the students of public policy who begin their analysis without establishing the nature of legitimacy for institutions, decision makers, or the regime itself commit a fundamental error in research. This is the context within which decisions are made and must be judged and considered as such.

23 Policy Implementation

A program consists of government actions initiated in order to secure objectives whose attainment is problematical. A program exists when the initial conditions – the "if" stage of the policy hypothesis – have been met. The initial premises of the hypothesis have been authorized. The degree to which the predicted consequences (the "then" stage) take place may be called implementation.

Implementation is the set of activities directed at putting a program into effect. Three of these activities are particularly important to successful implementation:

- Interpretation
- Organization
- Application

Interpretation is translating a program's language into specific plans, directives, and regulatory requirements.

Organization is the establishment of offices and methods, and the provision of resources for administering a program.

Application represents the routine provision of services, payments, or other program objectives or instruments.

Who is Involved?

The implementation system for any one program may be populated with a number of different types of actors so it is not easy to generalize. Those interacting for the purpose of putting a program into effect are involved in implementation. This generally includes bureaucrats, legislators, judges, private citizens, and private groups, who are all involved in implementation.

Techniques for Effective Implementation

There are some techniques that can make implementation more effective:

- Early Planning

- Scheduling Models
- Expediters, Incentives, and Participation
- Case Management
- Management By Objectives (MBO)

Early Planning: Early planning is important for policy implementation. These questions are what need to be asked: What action has to be taken? Who is to take it? Do these people have the capacity to do it?

Scheduling Models: These models facilitate the coordination of activities of an enterprise and help achieve a better utilization of resources. These models are useful for a wide range of activities, from the seemingly trivial task of scheduling a field office tour for high-ranking officials to the very complex technical job of scheduling intricate engineering processes. Three scheduling models are remarkable among the wide variety:

- Gantt Chart
- Critic Path Method (CPM)
- Program Evaluation Review (PERT)

Expediters, Incentives, and Participation: The expediter is a single individual or an organizational unit whose position is a way for top executives to demonstrate that things can work, that there is someone who can take rapid action, representing their office and getting things done. Incentives are rewards for helping to move the process along. Participation makes it clear where in the organization a certain answer to a question will be welcomed and when it will be resisted.

Case Management: Most of the resources of a public sector

organization are devoted to processing cases: patients in hospitals, welfare clients in a department of human resources, labor disputes in a labor relations board, grant proposals for a foundation, and so on. therefore, a focus on managing cases may yield more results.

Management By Objectives (MBO): MBO has four features:

- Establish overall objectives and priorities
- Encourage executives to contribute maximum efforts to attaining the overall objectives
- Coordinate planned achievement of all key objectives to promote greater total results for the whole organization
- Establish control mechanisms for monitoring progress compared to objectives and feed the results back to higher levels

Process of Influencing Implementation

External factors and internal factors affect implementation and are key in deciding whether it is successful.

External factors may skew the management effort and the implementing office cannot control many external factors. Among the most important external issues are:

– Political vulnerability
– Organizational location in the department
– Relations with industry/the legislature/the public

Political vulnerability: Pressure by the legislature, individual legislators, industry spokesmen, and individual operators, as well as by executive branch officials may produce a policy in reaction to specific crises, circumstances, and interests.

Organizational location in department: Many decisions are actually made in the top layers of an agency by approval of the head of the office. Office managers are never safe from a decision being reversed as a result of pressure from somewhere else in the government.

Relations with industry/the legislature/the public: Related groups may try to solve problems on a joint basis or there may be conflict and disagreement.

Internal Factors

Even if all external factors were removed, management problems would not be solved and better performance would not automatically follow. The central issues are:

- Lack of leadership
- Lack of clarity
- Lack of stability
- Lack of field perspective
- Lack of support
- External focus
- Waste of staff resources
- Lack of staff involvement
- Poor communication

Lack of leadership: No one is in charge of the office and the lack of strong direction leaves the operation vulnerable to whipsawing tactics of both the legislature and industry.

Lack of clarity: Confusion between the regulatory and educational functions creates problems that extend to the roles and functions of various staff members.

Lack of stability: Rearrangement of sections and changes of

supervisors create program as well as policy uncertainty.

Lack of field perspective: The office does not recognize the crucial nature of field activity operating from a top-down hierarchical approach.

Lack of support: Staff members, particularly in the field, feel isolated and receive little support from the central office.

External focus: External crises generated by pressures from the legislature and industry mean that the office chief pays little attention to program and personnel concerns.

Waste of staff resources: The office administration basically ignores professionals rather than use their experience and expertise.

Lack of staff involvement: Staff are not used for problem solving, and policy and program development or evaluation.

Poor communication: There is a lack of clearly-developed, articulated, and written policies throughout the system. Information sharing appears to be blocked to and from the field.

Implementation Approaches

There are three main eras of policy implementation research. The *first era* (1960s and early 1970s) was characterized by works such as Derthick (1972) and Pressman and Wildavsky (1973). These studies focused on individual cases and did not create more generalizable theory that could be applied to and tested with other cases.

The *second era* of implementation studies (mid-1970s) sought to create systematic theories of the policy process that were generalizable to many cases, rather than focused on one or few cases. This can be divided into two separate research approaches:

- *Top-down approach*
- *Bottom-up approach*

The first of these approaches emphasizes a *top-down* perspective of policy implementation. It claims that policy implementation can be understood by looking at the goals and strategies adopted in the statute or other policy, as structured by the implementers of policy. This focuses on the gaps between the goals set by a policy's drafters and the actual implementation and outcomes of the policy.

The top-down approach is based on a set of important assumptions:

- Policies contain clearly defined goals against which performance can be measured. According to Ryan (1995), "Top-down implementation strategies greatly depend on the capacity of policy objectives to be clearly and consistently defined."
- Policies contain clearly defined policy tools for the accomplishment of goals.
- The policy has a single statute or other authoritative statement of policy.
- There is an "implementation chain" that starts with a policy message at the top and other steps following like links in a chain.
- Policy designers have good knowledge of the capacity and commitment of the implementers. Capacity includes the availability of resources for an implementing organization to carry out its tasks. These include monetary and human resources, legal authority and autonomy as well as the knowledge needed to implement policy effectively. Com-

mitment includes the desire of the implementers to carry out the goals of policy designers. A high level of commitment means that the values and goals of the policy designers are shared by lower-level implementers such as teachers, police officers, or social workers.

The second approach emphasizes a *bottom-up* perspective, which suggests that implementation is best studied by starting at the lowest levels of the implementation system or chain and moving upward to see where implementation is more or less successful.

Bottom-up approaches recognize that goals are ambiguous rather than explicit and may conflict with other goals in the same policy area as well as with the norms and motivations of lower-level bureaucrats. Top-down models are most concerned with compliance, while bottom-up approaches value understanding how conflict can be overcome with bargaining and compromise.

The bottom-up approach does not require that there be a single defined policy in the form of a statute or other form. Rather, policy can be thought of as a set of laws, rules, practices, and norms that shape the ways government and interest groups address problems such as energy or crime. Thus, implementation can be viewed as a continuation of the conflicts and compromises that occur throughout the policy process, not just before and during enactment.

This bottom-up approach has a number of advantages. In particular, the lack of a focus on a specific program and a fixed top-to-bottom implementation chain means that the bottom-up approach can view implementation as working through a network of factors. This is much more like an issue network or policy community than a rigidly-specified process that fails to account for the richness of the policy-making environment.

On the other hand, there are also important shortcomings to consider in the bottom-up approach. First, the bottom-up approach overemphasizes the ability of low-level bureaucrats to frustrate the goals of top policy makers. Second, bottom-up models of implementation assume that groups are active participants in the implementation process even though this is not always true. The bottom-up approach also fails to take into account the power differences of target groups.

The third era: synthesis Researchers have sought to combine the benefits of the top-down and bottom-up approaches into one model or synthesis because of their relative strengths and weaknesses. They look for one model that can address both the structuring of policy from the top and the likelihood of its subversion or at least its alteration at the ultimate point of implementation. Sabatier (1991) argued that a conceptual framework should be developed that combines the best of the top-down and bottom-up approaches. The *top-down* approach is best where there is a dominant program (or law) that is well structured and where the researcher's resources for studying implementation are limited. The *bottom-up* approach is best when an analyst is interested in the dynamics of local implementation and where there is no single dominant program.

Sabatier's synthesis relies on a framework for studying public policy known as the Advocacy Coalition Framework, or ACF (see Week 4). Refining and reconciling the top-down and bottom-up approaches, Goggin et al. (1990) devised a theory of policy implementation that relies on sending messages between policy makers and implementers.

Regular staff meetings are used to encourage the free flow of ideas and information and to break down any isolation or distrust. Clearly articulated written policies and procedures are circulated to all staff members. Affected staff members hold regular discussions and reviews of draft regulations. Finally, there are expanded staff development and in-service training sessions.

What Can Be Done for More Effective Implementation?

Develop a consistent system of program and personnel review. Increase the visibility and accessibility of the head administrative officer. The office head and office managers can show clear indications of support for their staff, especially field staff, by asserting strong leadership, making the office mission clear, and instituting strong, consistent, and predictable management practices.

Program implementation is concerned with what happens to a policy or program after it has been formulated. Implementation is a complex process involving more than managing government programs. The principal concern is explaining how implementation can become successful. Implementation failures are more likely if the implementation structure includes organizations that have institutional interests and incentives that conflict with policy goals.

24 Policy Evaluation

Evaluation is the measurement of the desirable and undesirable consequences of actions taken to forward some goal. This includes:

– The procedures of gathering information about the results of planned social actions
– Measurement of the effectiveness of the program in terms of the fulfillment of the program's objective
– Describing the effects of a program and thereby make progressive adjustments in order to reach goals more effectively

The six main uses of an evaluation study are:

– To discover whether and how well objectives are being fulfilled
– To determine the reasons for specific successes and failures
– To uncover the principles underlying a successful program
– To direct the course of experiments with techniques for increasing effectiveness
– To lay the basis for further research on the reasons for the relative success of alternative techniques
– To redefine the means to be used for attaining objectives, and even to redefine goals in the light of research findings

These purposes strongly suggest an almost intrinsic relationship between evaluation and program planning and development. Evaluative research provides the basic information for designing and redesigning action programs. Some questions that need to be asked for a satisfactory evaluation include:

– What kind of change is desired?

- How is change to be brought about?
- What is the evidence that the changes observed are due to the means employed?
- What is the meaning of the changes?
- Were there unexpected consequences?

The major concern in evaluation is with the reliability and validity of the measures of effectiveness and with an understanding of the reasons for success or failure. Six steps are essential for evaluation:

- Identification of the goals to be evaluated
- Analysis of the problems the activity must address
- Description and standardization of the activity
- Measurement of the degree of change
- Determination whether the observed change is due to the activity or to some other cause
- Some identification of the durability of the effects.

Evaluation Process

Evaluation always starts with some value, either explicit or implicit. Then a goal is formulated based on this value. The selection of goals usually comes before or happens with value formation. A value may be defined as any aspect of a situation event, or object that is seen as being good, bad, desirable, or undesirable. Values are the principles by which people establish priorities and hierarchies of importance among needs, demands, and goals (Kingdon, 1995). Figure 8-6 illustrates the evaluation process.

Examples of goal-setting would be saying that fewer people should develop coronary disease, or that fewer people should die from cancer. Goal setting forces are always in competition with each other for money, resources, and effort. Next, there has to be some way of measuring goal attainment. If the goal is set that fewer people should die from cancer, then some means of discovering how many are presently dying from cancer is needed. The nature of the evaluation depends largely on the type of measures available to determine the attainment of objectives.

[Figure 8-6] The Evaluation Process

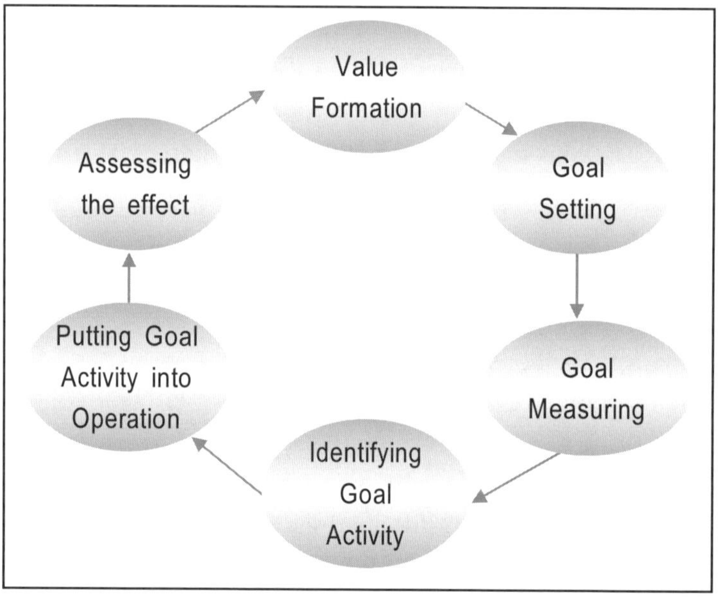

The next step in the process is identification of some kind of goal-attaining activity. In the case of cancer, for example, a program of early detection and treatment might be considered. Then the goal-attaining activity is put into operation. Diagnostic centers would be set up and people urged to come in for check-ups.

This goal-directed operation is assessed at some point. This stage includes the evaluation of the degree to which the operating program has achieved the predetermined objectives. This assessment may be done scientifically.

Finally, a judgment is made on the basis of the assessment as to whether the goal-directed activity was worthwhile. This brings the process back to value formation. People may now say that it is good to have cancer diagnostic centers. At the end of the evaluation process, there may be a new value, or the process may reaffirm, reassess, or redefine an old value.

Objectives and Assumptions

The most identifying feature of evaluation is the presence of some goal or objective whose measure of attainment constitutes the main focus of the research problem. Evaluation must have a goal. Some of the more general considerations involved in the formulation of objectives for evaluation include:

- What is the nature of the content of the objectives?
  Is the program interested in changing knowledge, attitudes, and/or behavior? Is it concerned with producing exposure, awareness, interest, and/or action? Answers to these questions permit the evaluator to determine within what regions the concepts are set.
- Who is the target of the program?
  At which groups in the population is the program aimed? Is the program seeking to change individuals, groups, or whole communities?
- When is the desired change to take place?
  Is the program seeking an immediate effect or gradually

building toward some postponed effect?

- Are the objectives unitary or multiple?

  Is the program aimed at a single change or at a series of changes? Are these changes the same for all people or do they vary for different groups of people?

- What is the desired magnitude of effect?

  Is the program seeking widespread or concentrated results? Does any particular proportion of effectiveness need to be attained before the program can be considered a success? Are there any specified standards of accomplishment that have to be met?

- How is the objective to be attained?

  What means are to be used to implement the program? Will the program depend primarily on voluntary cooperation or will an attempt be made to secure legal sanctions? Will personal or impersonal, formal or informal appeals be made?

These six considerations deal with basic questions that need to be answered in formulating the objectives of a program for the sake of evaluation.

Many of the answers to the questions raised above will require an examination of the underlying assumptions of the stated objectives. Assumptions may be divided into two types:

- Value assumption
- Validity assumption

Value assumptions pertain to the system of beliefs concerning what is good within a society or subgroup of society. There may be such almost universally accepted value assumptions as "human life is worth saving," "unnecessary suffering is bad," and "good health is desired."

Validity assumptions are much more specifically related to program objectives. Such assumptions, for example, underlie the belief that the cause for much prenatal morality may be found in lack of care during pregnancy and that prenatal clinics that supply information to expectant mothers can improve care and result in a reduction in prenatal mortality.

These validity assumptions help explain the move from mental institutions to home care based on the belief that people are better off at home than in institutions. The concepts of validity and reliability are important elements in the establishment of assumptions. Each assumption assumes the validity of an objective, meaning that each objective is valid for the achievement of some desired value.

Functions of Evaluation

Evaluation provides several functions that make it particularly useful to engage in the process.

Providing information: First and most important function of evaluation is providing reliable and valid information about policy performance, that is, the extent to which needs, values, and opportunities have been realized through public action.

Revealing particular goals: Evaluation reveals the extent to which particular goals and objectives have been attained and helps make practical inferences about the degree to which policy problems have been resolved.

Clarification and critique of values: Evaluation contributes to the clarification and critique of values that underlie the selection of goals and objectives. Values are clarified by defining and operationalizing goals and objectives. Values are also critiqued by questioning the appropriateness of goals and objectives in relation to the problem being addressed.

Creating alternative sources: In questioning goals and objectives, analysts may examine alternative sources of values (such as public officials, vested interests, and client groups) as well as their grounds in different forms of rationality (technical, economic, legal, social, substantive).

Contributing to other policy-analysis methods: Evaluation may contribute to the application of other policy-analysis methods, including recommendation and problem structuring. Information about inadequate policy performance may contribute to the restructuring of policy problems, for example, by showing that goals and objectives should be redefined.

Contributing to the definition of new or revised policy alternatives: Evaluation can also contribute to the definition of new or revised policy alternatives. For example, this can be done by showing that a previously favored policy alternative should be abandoned and replaced with another one.

Problems Approach and Experimentation

Evaluation is a technique for managing public organizations in which systematic data gathering and other research-like operations play a considerable role. From this angle, research-infused evaluation differs from other social research not in regard to the research designs and data – collection methods employed, but in the problems to be addressed. Problems, not designs or methods, provide the identity of evaluation.

There are eight primary evaluation problems. They can be expressed in the form of eight questions. Evaluators may consider some or all of the following eight problems:

- The purpose problem: What are the overall aims of the evaluation?
- The organization (evaluator) problem: Who should conduct the evaluation and how should it be organized?
- The intervention analysis problem: How is the objective of the evaluation to be characterized and described? Is the government intervention (normally a policy, a program, the components of policies and programs, or the provision of services and goods) regarded as a means or as a self-contained entity?
- The conversion problem: What does execution look like between the formal instigation of the intervention and the final outputs?
- The results problem: What are the outputs and outcomes - immediate, intermediate, and ultimate - of the intervention?
- The impact problem: What contingencies (causal factors, operating causal forces), the intervention included, explain the results?
- The criterion problem: What value criteria should be used to assess the merits of the intervention? What standards of performance can be used based on the value criteria to judge success or failure or satisfactory performance? What are the actual merits of the intervention?
- The utilization problem: How is the evaluation to be utilized? How is it actually used?

The first and second questions concern the evaluation of the intervention, three through seven are related to the intervention itself, and question eight concerns the feedback process.

Some Evaluation Techniques

Some techniques of evaluation such as Cost Benefit Analysis (CBA), Cost Effectiveness Analysis (CEA), and decision analysis have already been discussed. Here some other techniques are covered:

- Network analysis
- Linear programming
- Simulation

Network Analysis

Once a program or project has been decided, the problems of actually scheduling the components of the program remain: overtime, distributing resources to the various parts of the project, and rescheduling activities when conditions change. This phase of planning is especially difficult when dealing with non-repetitive tasks. These are jobs that have not been done before in exactly the same manner. Two similar network techniques have been developed for scheduling complex projects consisting of many interrelated tasks:

- Program Evaluation and Review Technique (PERT)
- Critical Path Method (CPM)

Program Evaluation and Review Technique (PERT) defines and links together the various tasks that must be done as part of a project in a sequenced network. Time estimates for the completion of each task are used to examine the various ways of changing individual task times to speed up the completion of the entire project.

Suppose a city park department wants to set up a neighborhood playground using volunteers and city employees.

The first step is to define the tasks or activities necessary to complete the project. Four activities are necessary to build the proposed playground: (1) the necessary materials and equipment must be purchased; (2) the site must be cleaned of trash and weeds; (3) the playground equipment must be installed; and (4) some landscaping must be done.

[Figure 8-7] A Simple PERT Network

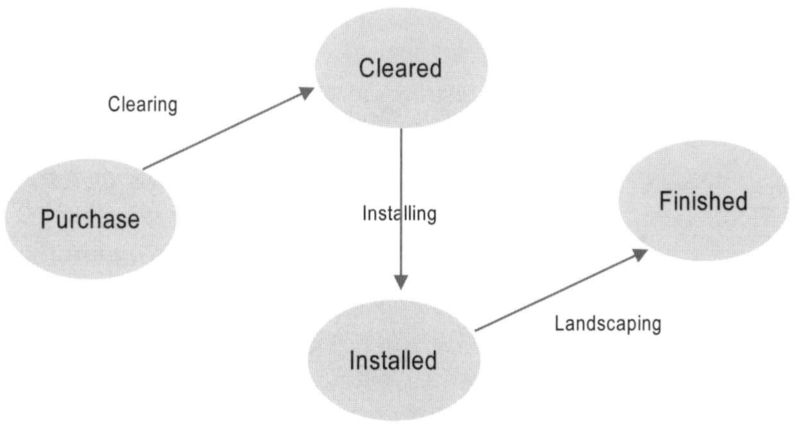

The second step is to place these activities in a functional sequence as in the figure. Activities are represented as lines with arrowheads that connect events. Events are the beginnings and endings of activities and are represented as circles. Each project begins and ends with a single event, and each activity has a beginning event and an ending event.

The third step consists of getting time estimates for each activity from the various work groups. Because getting only one time estimate is risky, three estimates are requested for each activity. The most optimistic time, or a, is the time it could take under the best conditions, the time likely to happen only one out of 100 times. The most pessimistic time, or b, is the time it would take under the worst conditions, a time also having a one percent probability of happening. The most likely time, or m, is the time expected to be the most common (modal) if the activity is repeated many times under many conditions. These estimates are then combined algebraically to calculate the expected time or t_e, as represented in the following formula:

$$t_e = \frac{a + 4m + b}{6}$$

This formula weights the most likely time (m) more heavily than both the most pessimistic time (b) and the most optimistic time (a), which are given the same weight. If there is only a one in 100 chance of b or a, then they should have less influence on t_e than m, the most likely time.

The fourth step is to determine the earliest date by which the project can be completed by figuring out the earliest expected date at which each activity can be finished.

Critical Path Method (CPM)

Like PERT, the critical path method uses networks and time estimates. CPM adds cost estimates to find the most efficient way of speeding up, or crashing, a project. The first steps are to estimate a normal time and a normal cost for each event and then to estimate a crash time and a crash cost for each activity.

Next step is to build the network and calculate t_e and the critical path, just as in PERT. Then the critical path is shortened by first crashing the activity with the cheapest crash cost. This provides a new time estimate for that activity, and the critical path is recalculated.

The next step is to un-crash the activities that do not lie on the critical path to the point where they become critical. Some of the crash projects have slack time and may be un-crashed to save money without changing the project completion date. Crashed activities are un-crashed until all are critical, a process that provides the optimum solution, the least cost, and minimum time to complete the project.

Who Can Do Evaluations?

Systematic evaluation studies are grounded in social science research techniques. Therefore most evaluation specialists have social science training. At first glance, someone unacquainted with evaluation research would undoubtedly find professional discussions of evaluation difficult to comprehend. As in any other professional field, evaluators have developed their own vocabulary, shorthand expressions, and rules for doing the work.

Some of the complexity of evaluation stems from the inherent tendencies of those in a professional field to develop their own language, but at least part of the need for special terminology derives from the unique concepts and insights developed in each field.

At the most complex level, evaluation activities can be so technically complicated, sophisticated in conception, costly, and of such long duration that they require the dedicated participation of highly-trained specialists at ease with the latest in social science theory, research methods, and statistical techniques. Such highly complex evaluations are usually conducted by specialized evaluators. At the other extreme, there are many evaluation tasks that can be easily understood and can be carried out by persons of modest expertise and experience.

However, students may sometimes mix the meaning of monitoring and evaluation. Monitoring is concerned with the production of designative claims and is therefore primarily concerned with establishing factual premises about public policies. Evaluation, by contrast, is a policy analysis procedure used to produce information about the performance of policies in satisfying needs, values, or opportunities that constitute a defined problem.

Models of Evaluation

Different models of evaluation may help understand more about the process. This section considers several such models.

Effectiveness Models

The greatest number of models fall under the category of effectiveness models. These include the goal attainment, comprehensive, client-oriented, and stakeholder models (see Figure 8-8).

Goal attainment evaluation: Goal attainment evaluation is an effectiveness model because it asks questions about the substantive content, output, and outcomes of the program, not about program procedures like equity of treatment or due process. It differs from economic and institutional models in that it raises substantive issues only, but neither pays heed to program costs nor to the organization of the evaluation.

Comprehensive evaluation: Comprehensive evaluation models are rooted in the conviction that evaluation should be more extensive than in the narrow goal-attainment model. The process of passing judgments should not be limited to achieved results but should at least include implementation and maybe even planning.

The first task of the evaluator in comprehensive evaluation is to contrast the intended results with the actual outcomes, the goals with the reality.

Client-oriented model: Proceeding from an entirely different point of departure, client-oriented evaluation takes the goals, expectations, concerns, or even needs of the program as its organizing principle and merit criteria. At the heart of the client oriented evaluation is the question of whether the program satisfies client concerns, desires, or expectations.

The stakeholder approach: The organizing principle of the stakeholder model is the concerns and issues of the people who have an interest in or are affected by the intervention. Stakeholder-based evaluation starts by mapping out the major groups who are involved or have an interest in the emergence, execution, and results of the program. The evaluator identifies the people who created the program, who initiated and funded it, and particularly those who are charged with its implementation.

Economic Models

Economic models include productivity and efficiency.

The productivity model can be expressed through the mathematical formula:

$$\text{Productivity} = \frac{\text{output}}{\text{input}}$$

Productivity has some technical advantages as a measure of public sector activities. Costs are sometimes not very difficult to calculate since they reach agencies in terms of money. However, it may be hard at other times to trace the relevant costs because the funds allocated and spent are often indicated on the books as lump sums. Outputs, on the other hand, may be exacting to catch and compute, even though productivity only presupposes that they are indicated in physical, not monetary, terms.

[Figure 8-8] Models of Evaluation

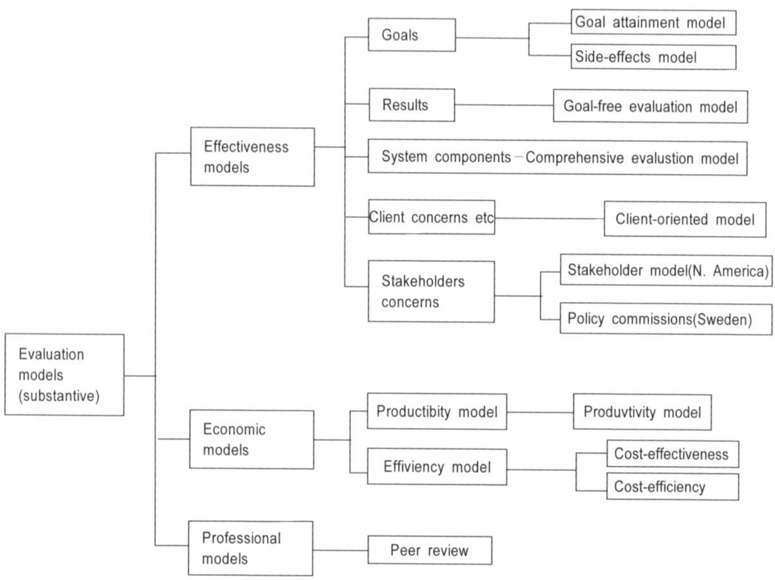

Efficiency can be measured in two ways, as cost-benefit or cost-effectiveness. Efficiency assessments provide a frame of reference for relating costs to program results. In cost benefit analysis, both program inputs and outcomes are measured in monetary terms. Inputs are estimated in monetary terms and outcomes in terms of actual impact in cost-effectiveness analysis.

[Figure 8-9] Cost-Benefit and Cost-Effectiveness

$$\text{Efficiency (cost-benefit)} = \frac{\text{Value of program effects (in KR won, US\$)}}{\text{costs (in KR won, US\$ etc.)}}$$

$$\text{Efficiency (cost effectiveness)} = \frac{\text{program effects in physical terms}}{\text{costs (in KR won\textbackslash, US\$ etc.)}}$$

Professional Models: Peer Review

The peer review mostly refers to a screening procedure for the selection of contributions to scientific journals. Submitted articles are subjected to peer review in order to decide whether they ought to be accepted for publication. Peer review is also used to offer guidance to research foundations concerning which projects should get funding. Research proposals are submitted to a group of respected colleagues for screening. On top of that, peer review has also been used to investigate and judge supposed transgressions of rules of ethical conduct and inherited research practices. This model is constantly used in research evaluation.

25 Policy Termination

Termination means ending, concluding, or cessation. Public policy termination is the deliberate conclusion or cessation of specific government functions, programs, policies, or organizations. Although termination represents the final step in the policy process, it should not conceptually be something to be considered last. The termination stage can be treated as both an end and a beginning: an end to a program that has served its purpose, and a beginning to correcting an errant policy or set of programs.

Types of "Policy" Termination

Generic policy termination uses the term "policy" to include government functions, organizations, and programs as well as policies themselves.

Functions: A function is defined as a service provided by a government for its citizens. It transcends organization and policies. A number of agencies and their respective policies can all serve the same function.

The relative performance of functions is not difficult to understand. Generally speaking, the government will only dispense with services or functions if society lacks either the assets or judgment to provide itself with necessary services. Economists have identified the category of "public goods" that can be considered governmental functions. National defense is a function that has outlived any number of reorganizations of the national defense establishment. Jurisdiction over regulatory matters and the redistribution of wealth and income are other instances of government functions. These functions or obligations are assumed by the government as a result of the demands of its citizens, and are instituted because they fill a need not otherwise met. Terminating them would therefore cause hardship and even suffering, the effects of which would spread outward through society. It is, therefore, not surprising that government tend to survive.

Organizations: Organizations are groups of individuals working together for a common purpose. Organizations are created to respond to specific needs although they may, and probably do expand their domain over time. They are designed to last and they do precisely that. Although organizations are rarely subjected to complete termination, it should be clear that they are more susceptible than governmental functions.

Policies: Organizations select and implement policies, which are generalized approaches or strategies toward solving particular problems. Although an organization can expend significant resources devising and executing appropriate policies, it should be stressed that policies are easier to terminate than the sponsoring organization itself.

This is true for four reasons. First, unless the policy and the institution are exactly coincident or inextricably interwoven, the organization will act to preserve itself before saving its components parts. The organization would prefer to forsake some of its policies rather than have the organization itself terminated. Second, a policy cannot usually find as many allies as the larger parent organization can. In the simple calculus of power politics, policies have fewer chips to expend on their survival. Third, policies are easier to evaluate relative to a given objective than an organization, which could have multiple policy objectives. Criteria are more available for the analyst to measure the policy's relative ineffectiveness and to support a case for termination. In this sense, it becomes much more vulnerable than the parent organization. Finally, most policies generate critics who can be expected to coalesce behind any termination proposal. Organizations, of course, also have a group of natural enemies. However, they are usually disposed against particular policies and therefore less likely to join a termination coalition against the organization. Policy may be the optimal level for an analyst to concentrate on termination.

Programs: Programs are the easiest of the four targets or levels of termination to end. Although they occupy the lowest stratum of the analyst's attention, individual programs have the fewest political resources to protect them and represent the smallest investment on the part of the organization. They are closest to the problem and therefore their impact can be most directly measured and, if found lacking, can most easily be blamed. On the other hand, the day-to-day minutia of program implementation might serve to shield them from the critical view of the analyst who may assume that the policy level is the appropriate focus of attention.

A Matter of Time

How does the tenure of an institution or policy affect termination? Although other variables can intervene, the longer a policy or institution has been existence, the more difficult it is in general to terminate. This condition is largely because of the allies are able to accumulate.

Termination is a rare political activity. The intellectual and political forces arrayed against termination are formidable. Unless the offending policy or organization is generally recognized as pernicious or dysfunctional, an analyst will have little initial support to justify a proposed termination. For these reasons, the termination process is seldom exercised unless the target is extremely weak and isolated without powerful allies or where the consequences of permitting a policy to continue were consensually seen to run directly counter to society's preferences.

Discussion Questions:

1. What is the process of agenda-setting?
2. Give an example of how different definitions of a problem can suggest different solutions.
3. What is the difference between routine, analogous, and creative policy formulation?
4. What is policy legitimation? Why is it important?
5. What are the techniques involved in policy implementation?
6. What are the steps in the process of evaluation? What are their functions?
7. Why is termination relatively rare?

Vocabulary

systematic agenda
institutional agenda
decision agenda
policy formulation
routine formulation
analogous formulation
creative formulation
formal policy actors
informal policy actors
legitimation
interpretation
organization
application
early planning
schedule models
expediters
incentives
participation
Case Management System
Management By Objectives
external factors
internal factors
political vulnerability
first era
second era
top-down approach

bottom-up approach
value assumption
validity assumption
network analysis
linear programming
simulation
Program Evaluation and Review Technique
Critical Path Method
productivity
efficiency
peer review

References

Allision, Graham. 1971. *Essence of Decision: Explaining the Cuban Missile Crisis.* Boston: Little, Brown.

Baumgartner, Frank and Jones, Bryan D. 1993. *Agendas and Instability in American Politics.* Chicago: University of Chicago Press.

Bendor, Jonathan and Hammond, Thomas H. 1992. "Rethinking Allison's Models." *American Political Science Review,* 86(2).

Berry, Jeffery M. 1989. "Subgovernments, Issue Networks, and Political Conflict." *Remaking American Politics.* Ed. Richard and Sidney Milkis Harris. Boulder, Colorado: Westview Press.

Birkland, Thomas A. 2001. *An Introduction to the Policy Process: Theories, Concepts, and Models of Public Policy Making.* New York: M.E. Sharpe.

Cigler, Allan J. 1991. "Interest Groups: A Subfield in Search of an Identity." *Political Science, Looking to the Future: Volume IV: American Institutions.* Ed. Evanston, Illinois: Northwestern University Press.

Cohen, Michael D., March, James G., and Olson, Johan P. 1972. "A Garbage Can Model of Organization Choice." *Administrative Science Quarterly,* 17:1-25.

Derthick, Martha. 1972. *New Towns in Town.* Washington, DC: Urban Institute.

Easton, David. 1965. *A Systems Analysis of Political Life.* New York: John Wiley.

Goggin, Malcolm L., Bowman, Anne O'M., Lester, James P., and O'Toole, Laurence J. 1990. *Implementation Theory and Practice: Toward a Third Generation.* Glenview, Illinois: Scott Foresman/Little Brown.

Kingdon, John W. 1995. *Agendas, Alternatives and Public Policies.* 2nd ed. New York: Harper Collins.

Kraft, Michael E. and Furlong, Scott R. 2004. *Public Policy: Politics, Analysis, and Alternatives.* Washington, D.C. CQ Press.

Lindblom, Charles E. 1959. "The Science of Muddling Through." *Public Administration Review*, 19: 79-88.

Majone, Giandomenico. 1989. *Evidence, Argument, and Persuasion in the Policy Process*. New Haven: Yale University Press.

Nakamura, Robert T. 1987. "The Textbook Policy Process and Implementation Research." *Policy Studies Journal*, 7(1): 142-154.

Neustadt, Richard E. 1990. *Presidential Power and the Modern Presidents: The Politics of Leadership from Roosevelt to Reagan.* New York: Free Press.

Peters, B. Guy. 1999. *American Public Policy: Promise and Performance.* Chappaqua, New York: Chatham House/Seven Rivers.

Pressman, Jeffrey and Wildavsky, Aaron. 1973. *Implementation.* Berkeley, CA: University of California Press.

Ryan, Neal. 1995. "Unraveling Conceptual Developments in Implementation Analysis." *Australian Journal of Public Administration*, 54(1): 65-81.

Sabatier, Paul A. 1991. "Political Science and Public Policy." *PS: Political Science and Politics*, 24(2): 144-147.

Vedung, Evert. 2005. *Public Policy and Evaluation Program*. New Brunswick, New Jersey: Transaction Publishers.

Zahariadis, Nikolaos. 1993. "To Sell or Not to Sell? Telecommunications Policy in Britain and France." *Journal of Public Policy,* 12(4): 355-376.

Week 9 Public Problems and Policy Alternatives

Summary

The creation of policy alternatives begins with the description of a problem. This is a problem of definition. Policy arguments may be decided on operational measures that are based on howa problem is defined.

Statistical information is abundantly available, but not everything can be reduced to quantitative measures. The future must also be anticipated.

The problem must be defined, measured, its extent and magnitude determined, its causes considered, goals set, and what can be done must be determined.

Most studies focus on the immediate causes of problems. Solving problems can begin with an explicit list of the goals of the various actors and possible ways of achieving those goals. Analysts look at costs and benefits and at how they are distributed.

Different alternatives include the things government has in its power to do. Government may regulate, subsidize, ration, tax and spend, contract out, use market incentives, privatize, charge fees, educate, hold in trust, and research. Assessing alternatives is a process of looking at criteria for evaluation.

26 Public Problems: Definition and Components

The beginning of any policy study involves description of a problem. Sometimes the problem, and perhaps even its causes, are obvious. For example, if the problem is teenage smoking and how to limit it, one can find abundant information about the number of teenage smokers, why they choose to smoke, and the implications for lifelong smoking habits and the associated health problems. Many governments use that information to adopt educational programs aimed at prevention and other policies that successfully reduce the rate of teenage smoking.

[Figure 9-1] Teenage Smoking is a Public Problem

Problem analysis involves trying to answer the basic questions about:

- The nature of the problem
- The extent or magnitude of the problem
- How the problem came about
- The major causes of the problem
- The importance of the problem as a public policy matter
- What the problem entails
- What is already known about the problem
- Possible solutions to the problem

Any copy of a daily newspaper contains information about a large number of potential policy problems such as crime, pollution, inflation, energy, welfare, and unemployment. Very few people argue that these are not problems, that is, that each of these conditions interferes with the attainment of some value or need. This may be personal security, health, consumption or some other desired state of affairs. Yet this everyday understanding of the meaning of problem is frequently inadequate, since it obscures the fact that the same problem (for example, crime) is viewed in radically different ways by different segments of the population. For some, crime is a natural condition of all human societies while for others it is an understandable response to poverty and exploitation. The way people view crime as a problem depends on several factors.

First, different people may agree that crime is a problem but may disagree about the kinds of behaviors that are criminal. One person may define crime solely in terms of illegal acts against people (homicide, armed robbery, rape) while another may focus on illegal acts involving property (theft, fraud, embezzlement, government corruption).

Second, people may also disagree about the kind/class of problem represented by criminal activities. Some people see crime as an economic problem. Therefore, the potential resolution lies in restructuring the production and distribution of goods and services in society. Others see it as a social, psychological, or even administrative problem that may be resolved by providing greater opportunities for social mobility, by changing attitudes through education, or by strictly enforcing existing criminal laws. The way people classify a problem generally determines the way they will explain and attempt to resolve it.

Finally, people may agree on the definition, classification, and explanation of a problem and yet disagree about its scope, severity, and importance. Judgments about the severity of a problem largely depend on what values and needs are deemed to be most important. People with a strong need for physical security, or those committed to values of law and order, are more likely to view crime as a policy problem than those with a strong commitment to social justice.

An essential step in the policy process is defining the problem. Definitions enable those seeking a solution to communicate with one another with a degree of precision that might not otherwise be possible. For example, analysts need to define what poverty means if they are studying the plight of the poor in Korea. Is being poor only a matter of having insufficient money or income, or does it include other characteristics, such as the lack of certain skills or abilities? Should poverty be defined in relative terms or in absolute terms?

Public policy arguments also depend on operational measures or operational indicators of problems. Rather than refer to poverty in the abstract, analysts want to know how many people live in poverty and their demographics. When discussing quality of education in the public schools, analysts want to see test scores and other student evaluations to determine whether a problem exists in the schools and how one community's schools compare to another's. If the subject is violent crime, the analysts need statistics about the number of crimes committed nationally and in local communities, and whether the crime rate is increasing or decreasing.

Quantitative measures are abundant for most contemporary public problems. How much statistical information needs to be provided is a matter of judgment. At a minimum, most issue papers or problem analyses include some basic descriptive statistics. One type is the frequency count, such as the percentage of the population at different income levels or the number of people in a survey who respond one way or another. Another type is the mean (average) measure of a group or category, such as the average score on an examination. An alternative is the median of a variable, which is the point where one half of the group is above and one half is below. One example is the median price of homes sold in different regions of the nation. Some idea of the range of variation or the correlation or relationship between two variables, such as age and income, may be useful as well.

Statistical information can be displayed in many ways in a report. These include tables that show frequency counts or percentages of what is being studied, such as the percentage of different age groups who smoke. Information can be superimposed on maps to show geographic variations such as rates of urban growth or the income levels for adjacent urban and suburban areas. Graphic figures such as pie charts or bar charts are common, as are line figures that show how the magnitude of a problem changes over time, such as the number of people without jobs from 1970 to 2000.

There is an art to choosing how best to display quantitative information. At a minimum, reports should aim for clarity. Even so, some visual displays are more likely to capture the reader's attention than others. The use of computer-generated color graphics allows a range of different formats, both in written form and in a PowerPoint or similar presentation. The best advice is generally to keep the audience and purpose clearly in mind when choosing the format of a report or presentation. The use of quantitative data also carries some risks. Analysts need to be alert to the possibility of inaccurate data in a report or an invalid measurement that does not truly capture the problem.

Naturally, not all human concerns, such as happiness or sense of well-being, can be reduced to quantitative measures. Analysts can, however, make use of surveys that ask people things like whether they are happy, enjoy living in their communities, and believe the schools are doing a good job. Where public problems can not be measured directly, this kind of survey may be useful substitute. Economists also say that people can be asked to estimate the dollar value of many activities for which no market value exists. Their responses can help to calculate whether certain actions, such as preserving open space or planting trees, are justifiable uses of tax dollars.

Anticipating the future

One other aspect of defining and measuring problems deserves mention. Any consideration of the present state of affairs must be grounded in an assessment of how a problem is likely to change over time. What will the problem look like in several years or decades? Forecasts, or projections, usually involve an extrapolation of current trends, but that is only one method for looking ahead.

Examples of forecasting include economic forecasting (will the nation have a surplus or deficit in five years?), population projections (how large will the country's population be by 2025 or 2050?), and energy needs (what kind, how much, and where?). Such projections are especially helpful if they reveal how that change will likely unfold with or without policy intervention. For example, to what extent would the nation adopting energy conservation measures reduce the reliance on imported oil?

Major Components of Public Problems

The flow chart in Figure 9-2 summarizes the basic elements of problem analysis. The list can also be a guide to what questions might be addressed in preparing a problem analysis or issue paper.

Define the problem

If the problem is educational quality, what does educational quality mean exactly? In other words, what is the exact nature of the education problem under the study? Has quality declined? Is it lower than many people believe it ought to be? Is it lower in the Republic of Korea than in other developed nations?

[Figure 9-2] Flow Chart of Problem Analysis

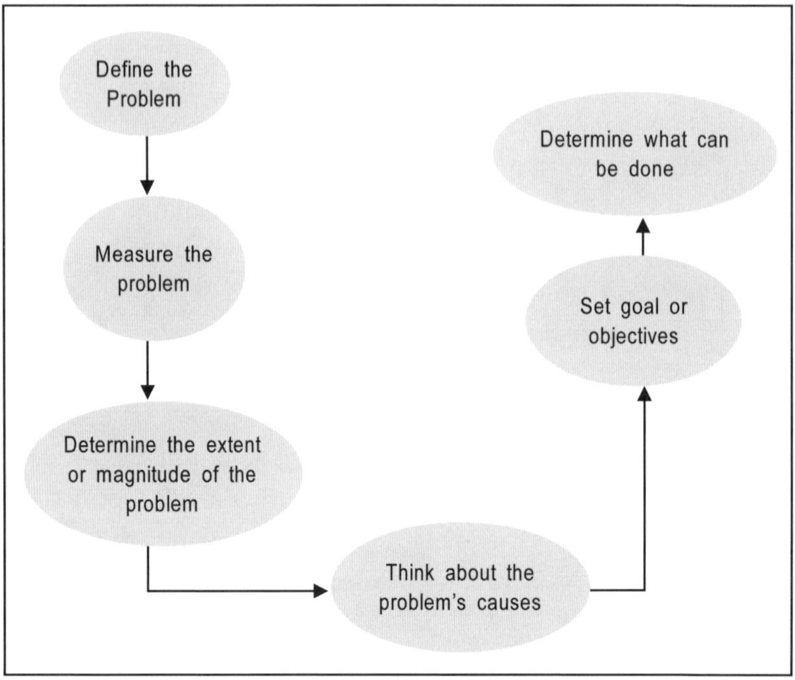

Measure the problem

Find a way to measure the problem that is consistent with the way it is defined. This step is sometimes called developing an operational definition. What kinds of quantitative indicators are available from reliable sources? What is the best measurement to use for educational quality? Student scores on standardized examinations? Other measures of student learning? Indicators of the quality of a school's faculty?

Determine the extent or magnitude of the problem

Using indicators that are available, try to determine who is affected by the problem and by how much. Try to answer these kinds of questions: what groups in the population suffer from the problem being studied, how long have they been affected by it, and to what extent are they affected? For example, how does educational quality vary from one school district or region to another? From urban districts to rural districts? From schools in less-affluent neighborhoods to those in more-affluent areas?

Think about the problem's causes

How did the problem come about, and why does it continue? What are the leading causes of the problem, and what other causes should be considered? Knowing the causes of a problem is critical to developing solutions to it. How has educational quality changed over the past several decades, and why?

Set goals or objectives

What should be done about the problem and why? Are certain goals and objectives of paramount importance, widely agreed upon, and economically or socially feasible? Over what period of time should the goals and objectives be sought? For educational quality, what goals or objectives are most appropriate? If quality is to be improved, how much progress should be expected for a given period of time?

Determine what can be done

What actions might work to solve the problem or reach the specified goals and objectives? What policy efforts might be directed at the causes of the problem? What variables can be affected by such efforts? If the goal is improving educational quality to a certain extent, what needs to be done? Improving teacher quality? Reducing class sizes? Changing the curriculum?

[Figure 9-3] Structure of Policy Problems

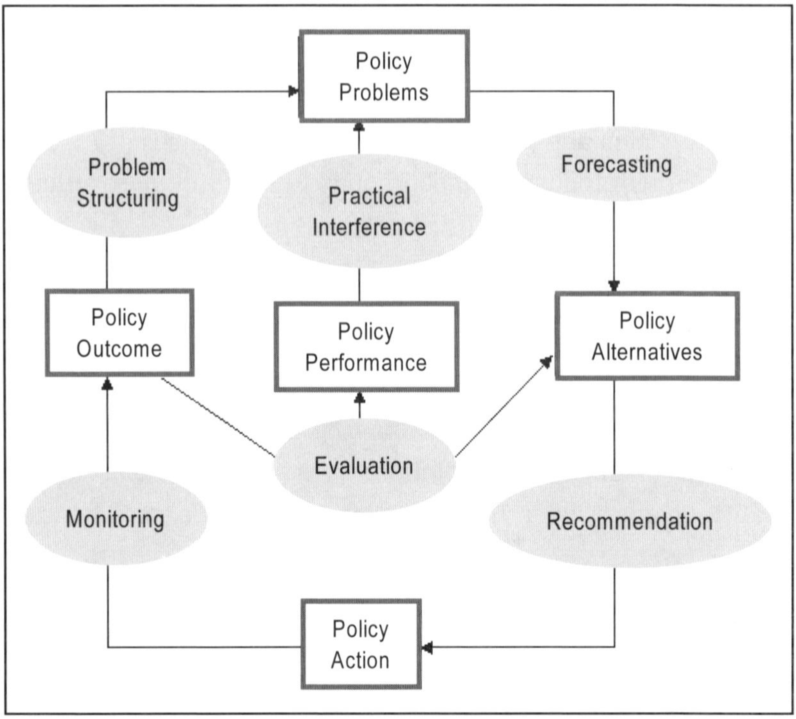

Thinking about Causes and Solutions

Any assessment of a public problem requires thinking about its causes, how it came about, and why it continues. The answers make a big difference in whether and how public policy might resolve the problem. For example, if the question is why youth unemployment increased dramatically from 1996 to 2015, part of the answer is that employment security overall decreased through the period. In many companies, there even have been mass layoffs of long-term employees. If there is a general problem in job security, there is likely to be a specific problem for youth as well.

Most policy studies focus on what can be called proximate, or immediate, causes of public problems. The greater challenge is to deal with the root causes of problems. Taking policy action might be more difficult because of long-standing public attitudes and habits that are resistant to change. Think about urban traffic congestion. Why does it exist? The obvious answer is that too many people are driving their cars on a limited number of roads at any given time. Is the solution to build more highways? Or is it to think about ways to reduce the use of automobile in urban areas where congestion is greatest? Some urban designers and environmentalists offer a more radical solution, at least for new communities. They suggest building cities with adequate mass transit where people can live closer to where they work. Many states and communities are adopting "smart growth" policies with similar ambitions for managing anticipated growth over the next several decades.

Most public problems have multiple causes, and therefore people disagree over which is the most important and which ought to be the object of public policy. The astute student of public policy learns how to deal with the politics and overheated rhetoric that can sometimes cloud an objective review of the evidence.

Public problem solving can begin with making an explicit list of the goals and objectives of various policy actors and a determination of what might be done to reach them. The objectives may include a specific measure of what is to be achieved, such as improving access to health care services or reducing the rate of teenage smoking. When analysts think of potential solutions to public problems, they try to identify the opportunities for policy intervention. They try to imagine how a change in public policy might affect the problem. For example, would raising the price of cigarettes reduce the teenage smoking rate?

Analysts sometimes want to describe the benefits and costs of trying to solve a problem. They look at how the consequences of policy action, positive or negative, are distributed across population subgroups, such as those in certain regions, occupations, or social groups – in other words, who gains and who loses if the problem is resolved. Politicians and other major policy actors are sometimes very clever about addressing these kinds of distributive concerns. They are almost always interested in knowing about them. They may speak about solving public problems as though the entire nation will benefit equally, but the reality is that some segments of the population are more likely than others to enjoy the benefits of acting on a problem, and some are more likely than others to pay the costs. It is wise to think about how to present such information.

27 Constructing Alternatives

Constructing alternatives focuses on how to develop the list of alternatives that merit further consideration. It emphasizes learning how to think creatively about public policy, particularly when ineffective policies and programs need to be replaced. How do analysts know which alternatives to consider?

What Can Governments Do?

The starting point for constructing alternatives is to see what governments are doing or can do. Among their options, governments can regulate, subsidize, ration, tax and spend, contract out, use market incentives, privatize, charge fees for service educate, create public trust, and commission research. Table 9-1 summarizes these activities and illustrates them with examples.

Analysts might suggest modifying the present policies or trying a different policy approach or strategy when current policies are not working well enough and a change is needed. Present policy could be strengthened. For example, the national government could raise standards for clean air or water policies. Policy makers could fund programs at a higher level, which might permit improved research, better enforcement, and better public information campaigns. Analysts and policy makers also consider alternatives to conventional regulatory policies. This might include a combination of market-based incentives, public information campaigns, and various forms of regulatory reinvention, which are more flexible and efficient policy reforms.

For some policies and agencies policy makers might try different institutional approaches, such as a new way to organize the bureaucracy in charge. For example, the Korean Ministry of Culture was split off of the Ministry of Culture and Information in 1990, and became the Ministry of Culture and Tourism in 1998, and is currently the Ministry of Culture, Sports and Tourism.

[Table 9-1] What Can Governments Do?

Action	Illustrations	Specific Examples
Regulate	Licensing, inspection, enforcement of standards, application of sanctions.	Environmental, health, and workplace safety regulation; corporate financial regulations.
Subsidize	Loans, direct payments or benefits, tax credits, price supports.	Student loans, subsidies to farmers; low interest loans for disaster recovery.
Ration	Limit access to scarce resources.	Charge fees for museum entrance; limit services covered by national health insurance.
Tax and spend	Tax an activity at a level that encourages or discourages it. Spend money on preferred programs.	Allowing insurance deductions to encourage purchase; imposing cigarette taxes to discourage smoking. Defense weapons, prisons, public higher education.
Contract out	Contract government services from the private sector or buy products for government agencies.	Defense contracts for weapons procurement; purchase of computers and fleet vehicles for federal or state governments or public schools.
Use market incentives	A special category of taxation or imposition of fees that creates incentives for changing behavior and achieving goals and objectives.	Raising gasoline taxes to encourage conservation of fuel and reduce carbon dioxide emissions; tax rebates for purchasing hybrid vehicles
Privatize	Transferring public services from government to the private sector.	Turning over management of public schools to private companies.

Charge fees	Fees for select services.	Requiring students to pay to ride the school bus; charging for parking at public facilities.
Educate	Provide information to the public through formal programs or other actions.	Formal public meetings; public education services; food safety labels; information on toxic chemical releases; automobile fuel efficiency labels.
Create public trusts	Holding public property in trust for citizens indefinitely.	Local land conservation trusts, state and national parks and recreation areas.
Conduct research	Conduct or support research and development.	Support for government research institutes and think tanks.

Governments are trying another interesting institutional reform option. They make routine government services available online, everything from providing tourists information to supplying government forms that people can fill out on their computers. Governments report improved efficiency, and the users say they are more satisfied with the results and think more highly of the agencies than before.

Actions in many policy areas are rooted in one of two views of the problem being confronted. These might be called the supply and demand perspectives. If analysts believe a problem such as energy scarcity results from an insufficient supply of energy, they would likely recommend the policy alternative of increasing supply. They would consider actions to boost supplies of energy, whether from fossil fuels (oil, natural gas, and coal), nuclear energy, or alternative energy such as wind or solar power. Conversely, the demand perspective would recommend addressing demand. To consider which policy option will work best or be more efficient or fair, policy makers also have to think about the philosophical and ideological aspects.

28 Assessing Policy Alternatives

Assessing policy alternatives is about applying evaluative criteria. Analysts have many ways to present the alternatives so that policy makers and other interested parties can understand the analysis and the choices they face. For example, if three policy options are offered for consideration, the analyst might present each in terms of its likely effectiveness, economic efficiency, and equity. Trade-offs are inevitable in this kind of decision making. Only rarely does a particular policy option rank highest on all of the evaluative criteria. It is far more likely that one option is judged to be most effective, but another cheaper or more equitable in its effects. Analysts, therefore, attach weight to each criterion. For example, is equity more important than efficiency in promoting cleanup of hazardous waste sites? Should governments clean up the most dangerous sites first or try to ameliorate the conditions at several sites at once? Or should the resources be directed to sites that have a disproportionate impact on poor and minority communities? Would doing so promote greater equity? As analysts consider more than a few conflicting bases for assessing policy options, the necessity for weighting criteria increases.

Discussion Questions:

1. Why is the process of problem definition important?
2. What are the major components of public programs?
3. What are the different categories of alternatives?
4. How are policy alternatives assessed?

Vocabulary

quantitative
qualitative
statistics
goal
objective
proximate causes
regulatory reinvention

References

Anderson, James E. 2003. *Public Policy Making.* 5th ed. Boston: Houghton Mifflin.

Birkland, Thomas A. 2001. *An Introduction to the Policy Process: Theories, Concepts, and Models of Public Policy Making.* New York: M.E. Sharpe.

Dunn, N. William. 1981. *An Introduction Public Policy Analysis.* Englewood Cliffs, New Jersey: Prentice-Hall, Inc.

Kraft, Michael E. and Furlong, Scott R. 2004. *Public Policy: Politics, Analysis, and Alternatives.* Washington, D.C. CQ Press.

Patton, Carl V. and Sawicki, David S. 1993. *Basic Methods of Policy Analysis and Planning.* 2nd ed. Englewood Cliffs, New Jersey: Prentice Hall.

Starling, Grover. 1988. *Strategies for Policy Making.* Chicago: Dorsey Press.

Ringquist, Evan J. 1993. *Environmental Protection at the State Level: Politics and Progress in Controlling Pollution.* Armonk, New York: M. E. Sharpe.

Week 10 Creative Thinking about Policy Action

Summary

Analysts may go beyond policy typologies and variations on existing policies. They may also gather ideas through brainstorming. They may do quick surveys. They may conduct literature reviews to discover what is known about a problem. They may also compare existing situations against some ideal standard.

Beyond considering policy typologies or variations on existing policies analysts can try other techniques to expand their list of policy alternatives. Here the discussion is centered on how to apply creative thinking on policy action. Among other strategies some scholars suggest the following: no-action analysis, quick surveys, literature reviews, comparison to real world situations, passive collection and classification, use of analogies and metaphors, brainstorming, and comparison with an ideal. This chapter will discuss:

- Brainstorming
- Quick surveys

– Literature reviews
– Comparison with an ideal

29 Brainstorming

Brainstorming is a method for generating ideas, goals, and strategies that help identify and conceptualize problematic situations. It may be used to generate a large number of suggestions about potential solutions for problems.

Brainstorming is a popular technique for encouraging creative thinking in public policy or in organizational change. It usually takes place in an informal meeting of people who share an interest in finding solutions to a given problem.

The participants in a brainstorming session bounce ideas around with the goal of producing a list of possibilities. Ideas are offered and recorded as they are made, with no attempt to criticize or evaluate them. This freewheeling discussion of the issues should produce creative thinking and numerous suggestions. In the second phase of the meeting, the participants reduce the number of suggestions to come up with a shorter list of alternatives worthy of further consideration.

Brainstorming can also take the form of written suggestions rather than an open meeting with verbal responses. Some variations on the brainstorming theme suggest that creativity is enhanced when some structure is introduced into the discussions.

Brainstorming involves several simple procedures:

– Brainstorming groups should be composed in accordance with the nature of the problematic situation being investigated. This usually means the selection of particularly knowledgeable experts.

- The process of idea generation and idea evaluation should be kept strictly apart, since intense group discussion may be inhibited by premature criticism and debate.
- The atmosphere of brainstorming activities should be kept as open and permissive as possible in the idea - generating phase.
- Idea evaluation should begin only after the first phase of generating ideas has been exhausted.
- The group should prioritize ideas at the end of the idea-evaluation phase and incorporate them into a proposal that contains a conceptualization of the problem and its potential solutions.

Brainstorming is a highly versatile procedure that may involve relatively structured or unstructured activities, depending on the analyst's aims and the practical constraints of the situation. Relatively unstructured brainstorming activities occur frequently in government agencies and public and private "think tanks."

The main difference between brainstorming and other techniques for problem structuring is that the focus is on collective groups of experts rather than on individuals. Moreover, brainstorming activities are assessed, not in terms of logical consistency or the plausibility of comparisons, but according to consensus among members of brainstorming groups.

30 Quick Surveys

Quick surveys involve talking with people in a particular policy network or searching through hearings transcripts, minutes of meetings, newspaper accounts, and the like for pertinent information about a problem and policy alternatives. The idea here is that people familiar with the issues have probably raised many alternatives. Interviewing them, distributing questionnaires to them, or reviewing what hey have written or said on the issues should produce a short list of possible policy alternatives. This technique could be particularly useful at the local level where gaining access to principal policy actors is a real possibility.

31 Literature Review

A literature review is an examination of library sources such as books, journal articles, in addition to other sources like internet sites. The purpose here is to look for policy alternatives that have been proposed or considered previously. This kind of search could extend to a survey of the options that policy makers have considered or adopted in other policy area as well.

For example, the Korean Environmental Impact Assessment Act required that government agencies conduct an environmental impact analysis, and make it public, before making a major decision such as building highways. Can an impact analysis be applied elsewhere? In other words, why not require that specific studies or reports be conducted and made public prior to reaching a final decision in other areas of public policy?

Rather than think about abstract ideas, analysts might ask what has worked well in specific or real world situations, and therefore what might be considered an effective policy alternative for the present policy. Analysts also want to know which alternatives have been tried elsewhere and found wanting. Analysts can look to and evaluate what other nations have tried to do about a particular problem.

[Figure 10-1] The Library is Good Source of Information

32 Comparison with an Ideal

Analysts sometimes compare policy alternatives with an ideal situation. For example, as part of smart growth planning or sustainability efforts, many communities hold "visioning" meetings at which residents are encouraged to think about the community they want for the future. What kind of residential neighborhoods, what kind of downtown, what kind of recreational opportunities? The goal is to envision an ideal future and use that vision to generate ideas for moving in the desired direction.

Participants in public policy debates too often assume that

an ideal situation is unattainable and therefore not worthy of consideration. However, excluding ideals guarantees that they will be never come about. By encouraging the expression of an ideal, analysts can ensure that at least the more pragmatic ideas that do receive consideration are evaluated in terms of how close they come to the ideal.

Any of these strategies for generating a list of policy alternatives should help an analyst think clearly about how to solve a problem. At this point in the process, neither the cost nor the political feasibility of a particular option is the primary concern. Rather, the goal is to think critically about the problem and try to imagine the various ways of addressing it.

Discussion Questions:

1. How should brainstorming be conducted to be most effective?
2. When are quick surveys the most useful? How should they be conducted?
3. What is the purpose of a literature review? Where should a policy analyst look in order to conduct one?
4. What kinds of ideals can be the basis for a policy comparison?

Vocabulary

brainstorming
quick surveys
literature reviews
comparison with an ideal
questionnaire
transcripts
environmental impact
visioning

References

Birkland, Thomas A. 2001. *An Introduction to the Policy Process: Theories, Concepts, and Models of Public Policy Making.* New York: M. E. Sharpe.

Baumgartner, Frank R., and Jones, Bryan D. 1993. *Agendas and Instability in American Politics.* Chicago: University of Chicago Press.

Dunn, N. William. 1981. *An Introduction Public Policy Analysis.* Englewood Cliffs, New Jersey: Prentice-Hall, Inc.

Goldenberg, Jacob, David Mazursky, and Sorin Solomon. 1999. "Creative Sparks." *Science,* 3 (September): 1495-1496.

Kraft, Michael E. and Furlong, Scott R. 2004. *Public Policy: Politics, Analysis, and Alternatives.* Washington, D.C.: CQ Press.

Patton, Carl V. and Sawicki, David S. 1993. *Basic Methods of Policy Analysis and Planning.* 2nd ed. Englewood Cliffs, New Jersey: Prentice-Hall, Inc.

Week 11 Policy Failure, and Learning from It

Summary

Explanations for policy failure are complicated. Success and failure are not precise concepts. They are highly subjective and are related to the goals of the different policy actors.

Policies may fail due to untried alternatives, the impact of changing circumstances, the relationship between policies, political boundaries, excessive policy demands, unrealizable expectations, the inaccuracy of causal theories, the choice of policy tools, the complexity of the implementation process, and the failure of political institutions.

Analysts should learn from the failure of policies. Instrumental policy learning concerns the viability of policy designs and tools. Social policy learning concerns the social construction of policies. Political learning is about political strategy.

33 Explanations for Policy Failure

No doubt you have complained and heard others complain that a policy has failed. A lot of people complain about traffic congestion and public transportation. Why might a policy be a failure? It might be argued that there are not enough roads, or that the bus fare is too high. Maybe gas prices are not high enough to discourage automobile use and public transportation is not convenient enough.

[Figure 11-1] Public Transportation is a Success to Some and a Failure to Others

Ingram and Mann (1980) provided a number of useful ways to think about policy failure. They argued that "success and failure are slippery concepts, often highly subjective and reflective of an individual's goals, perception of need, and perhaps even psychological disposition toward life." In other words, failure is often in the eye of the beholder. Further, it is affected by immediate perception of the policy in question. One person might argue that a policy has failed, while another person might look at it as a tentative first step toward a larger goal. The current level of public transportation may have failed

[Table 11-1] Explanations for Policy Failure

Alternatives to policies tried	Failure needs to be assessed in terms of the do nothing option and in terms of the likelihood that other options would have been more or less successful.
The impact of changing circumstances	Changing circumstances can render policies less successful, such as energy policies that provide price relief before they create dependency on oil and natural gas.
Relationships of one policy to another	Policies are related and these relationships must be taken into account. For example, a stricter policy against unauthorized immigrants may endanger broader policy goals surrounding Korea's relations with China, such as trade or security.
The boundary question	Political boundaries (between provinces, for example) influence policy success.
Excessive policy demand	People may expect too much from policies.
Realizable policy expectations	Policies sometimes fail when they go beyond what can be achieved now though ambitious policy making can be the result of 'speculative argumentation' that seeks to induce innovation. The stated purpose of a policy may not be the actual purpose. There may be more symbolic goals than substance.
Accurate theory of causation	Policy will fail if it is not based on sound causal theory.
Choice of effective policy tools	The choice of ineffective tools will likely yield failure. However, the choice of tools is often a function of compromise or ideological predisposition.
The vagaries of implementation	The problems inherent in policy implementation can contribute to policy failure.
Failure of political institutions	Policy failure is a symptom of problems within political institutions such as the breakdown of political party power or devolution of power from legislative leaders to the committees and subcommittees.

some, but another person may think it just needs more support. Ideology plays a role. Conservative successes are often liberal failures and vice versa.

Other reasons for policy failure are listed in Table 11-1. If you are active in politics and policy making or even reasonably attentive to politics, you may recognize these reasons for policy failure. There are many possible reasons policy failure and many possible problems that can cause or contribute to policy failure. Thus, simple storytelling about policy failure may reflect popular dissatisfaction with a policy in particular, or government in general, but fails to take into account the multiple reasons why policies can at least be perceived as failures.

34 Policy Success, Failure, and Learning

Given that policies fail or at least appear to fail relatively often, it is likely that some sort of policy change will result from these failures if failure provides an opportunity to learn from mistakes. It is useful to think about how policy failure induces policy change through a learning process. Indeed, many experts and commentators on important public issues claim that certain phenomena can induce organizations to learn from their mistakes.

Bennet and Howlett (1992) note that learning can be a more active and "deliberate attempt to adjust the goals and techniques of policy in the light of the consequences of past policy and new information so as to better attain" policy goals. Indeed, organizations make concerted efforts to improve their learning capacity by creating systems to store and disseminate information. Sabatier (1988) provides a more specific definition of policy-oriented learning as "relatively enduring alternations of thought or behavioral intentions which result from experience and which are concerned with the attainment (or revision) of policy objectives."

You can think of learning at the organizational and individual level, but it is most useful to consider people as the agents of learning. People apply what they have learned in group policy-making processes.

Types of Learning

May (1990) divides learning into three categories:

- Instrumental policy learning
- Social policy learning
- Political learning

Instrumental policy learning concerns learning about the "viability of policy interventions or implementation designs" (May, 1990). This sort of learning centers on implementation tools and techniques. Learning seems to have happened and been successful when feedback from implementation is analyzed and changes to the design are made that improve its performance.

Social policy learning involves learning about the social construction of a policy or program. This type of learning goes beyond simple adjustments of program management to the heart of the problem itself, including attitudes toward program goals and the nature and appropriateness of government action. Social policy learning can result in better understanding of the underlying casual theory of a public problem if successfully applied, leading to better policy responses.

Three-Day Weekend Korea usually observes public holidays on a specific date. The public is lucky and gets a three-day weekend if the date happens to fall on a Monday or Friday. Otherwise, they get whatever day of the week off the date happens to fall on. On the other hand, the US observes most public holidays on a Monday so as to create a three-day holiday for citizens to enjoy a longer block of time off. Another effect of this is that these three-day weekends tend to generate substantial business, with American stores throwing special President's Day, Labor Day, and even Memorial Day and Veteran's Day sales that generate more economic activity. Following the big decline in retail sales and tourist revenue following the scare over the outbreak of MERS in the spring of 2015, President Park took advantage of the 70th anniversary Liberation Day on August 15, 2015 (8 · 15) to extend special observations to August 14, a Friday. This was done in part with the hope that the three-day weekend observing such a significant national event would give a shot to the economy and turn around some of the retail sales slump. Maybe Koreans will enjoy more three-day weekends in the future. *JoongAng Daily*

There are many examples of social policy learning. One example concerns the way the government addresses corruption. The government traditionally tried to control corruption by arresting offenders, and doing so often enough to dissuade people from taking or giving bribes. Newer methods like the OPEN procurement system have used information technology to decrease the opportunity for corruption while opening up government systems to greater transparency.

Political learning is considerably different from instrumental and social learning. Political learning involves learning better strategies for advocating for or against particular policies. Political learning is learning about effective political advocacy. It can be assumed to have occurred when advocates for or against policy change alter their strategy and tactics to conform to new information that has entered the political system.

Given the complexity of the Korean political system, it seems that policy failure would be the inevitable outcome of any public program. This may not be true, however, because failure is, like so much else in public policy, a subjective condition that is more often grounded in the perceptions of a particular interest than in empirical "fact." However, it can be stipulated that some policies are much less successful than others and that policy makers and others concerned with the management of public programs will learn from the purported failure of a policy. In this way, policy development is an ongoing process with no discernible beginning and no obvious end, but with plenty of opportunities for refinement and fine-tuning.

Discussion Questions:

1. Why do some policies fail?
2. Should policy standards be objective or subjective?
3. What can be learned from policy failure?
4. How can policy failure contribute to political development?

Vocabulary

alternatives to policies tried
the impact of changing circumstances
relationships between policies
the boundary question
excessive policy demand
realizable policy expectations
accurate theory of causation
choice of effective policy tools
the vagaries of implementation
failure of political institutions
instrumental policy learning
social policy learning
political learning

References

Anderson, James E. 2000. *Public Policy Making*. 4th ed. Boston: Houghton Mifflin.

Birkland, Thomas A. 2001. *An Introduction to the Policy Process: Theories, Concepts, and Models of Public Policy Making*. New York: M. E. Sharpe.

Bennet, Colin J. and Howlett, Michael. 1992. "The Lessons of Learning: Reconciling Theories of Policy Learning and Policy Change." *Policy Sciences*, 25 (3): 275-294.

Ingram, Helen and Mann, Dean. 1980. "Policy Failure: An Issues Deserving Attention." In *Why Policies Succeed or Fail*. Ingram, Helen, and Mann, Dean. ed. Beverly Hils, California: Sage.

Kang, Jin-Kyu. 2015. "3-Day Weekend for Liberation Day." Korea JoongAng Daily. August 5, 2015, from http://koreajoongangdaily.joins.com/news/article/Article.aspx?aid=3007504

Kraft, Michael E. and Furlong, Scott R. 2004. *Public Policy: Politics, Analysis, and Alternatives*. Washington, D.C. CQ Press.

May, Peter. 1990. "Reconsidering Policy Design: Policies and Publics." *Journal of Public Policy*, 11 (2): 187-206.

Ryan, Neal. 1995. "Unraveling Conceptual Developments in Implementation Analysis." *Australian Journal of Public Administration*, 54 (1): 65-81.

Sabatier, Paul A. 1988. "An Advocacy Coalition Framework of Policy Change and the Role of Policy-Oriented Learning Therein." *Policy Sciences*, 21: 129-168.

Week 12 Policy Capacity and Participation

Summary

Policy analysts can improve the performance of government and its responsiveness to citizens. The commonplace criticisms of government are based on popular assessments and not on objective evidence, which usually shows that government is functioning well. The policy process can help strengthen the capacity for citizens to participate in the public sphere.

35 Improving Policy Capacity

Policy analysis can help improve the performance of government and its responsiveness to citizen concerns. Now might be as good a time as any to consider how to improve the policy capacity of government. Public trust and confidence in government in Korea has fallen since early enthusiasm for democratization. Recent moves towards greater participation in government have increased government openness and yet elections still feature declining turnout.

Citizens have been troubled by continuing divisiveness in politics, the ethical failures of political leaders, and the inability of leaders to deliver an economy that meets the expectations of regular citizens. At the same time, these comparisons are against ideal situations. When government performance is judged against measurable criteria, its performance evaluation is often much better.

How can policy analysis contribute to improving the policy capacity of government? One way is through the analysis of proposed institutional reforms, such as changes in the electoral process, campaign finance, term limits for legislators, and opportunities for citizens to participate in decision making. This is a task at which political scientists excel. Yet their analysis too often fails to reach the public or even policy makers, who then act without the benefit of what analysis has uncovered.

Policy capacity can also improved through better evaluation of the agencies charged with implementing policies and programs. Evaluation of government institutions and processes sometimes comes from citizen groups.

One of the central tasks for improving government policy capacity is in the hands of the people. Government will continue to respond to organized groups and special interests if citizens lack interest in public affairs and fail to educate themselves on the issues. What citizens see as faulty performance in government sometimes reflects the influence of organized groups that work to ensure that policies affecting their operations are not effective or that they inflict minimum constraints on their activities. The best way to counter self-serving actions by special interests is for citizens to get involved.

36 Citizen Participation in Decision Making

The decision-making process affects what kinds of decisions are made and, ultimately, what impacts they have on society. Policy outcomes reflect who participates in the process, who does not, and the different resources that each policy actor brings to the decision-making arena. Public policies in a democracy maybe expected to be consistent with public preferences and meet the needs of citizens. As noted, however, policy makers are often more responsive to organized interests such as big private companies and industries than they are to the general public.

[Figure 12-1] Citizen Participation Improves Policy Capacity

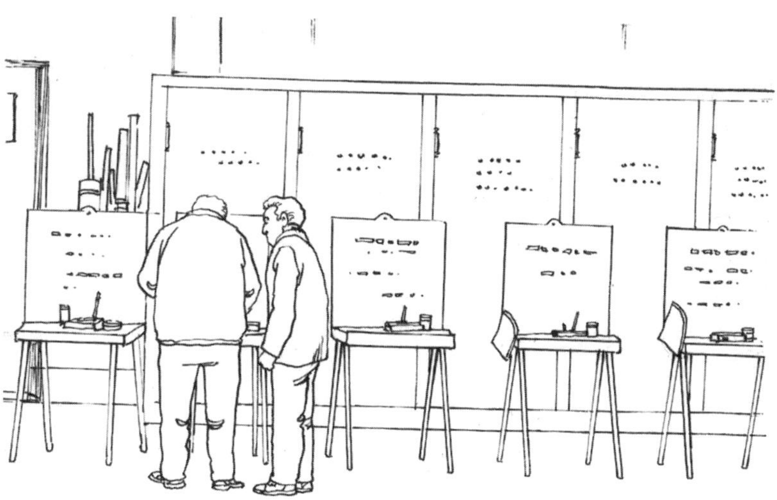

One way to overcome this is to strengthen citizen capacity to participate in policy making processes. The level of public participation in policy processes, whether voting in elections or taking an active role in civic affairs, has declined over the past several decades. Of all age groups, the youngest, including college students, have the lowest level of interest in politics and policy making and have the least active participation in these processes. It remains clear that citizen participation has a long way to go to be truly effective.

[Figure 12-2] The Jongno District Facility for Addressing Citizen Complaints is One Way of Encouraging Citizen Participation

Public participation in the policy process can go well beyond voting, writing letters or e-mail messages to policy makers, and

talking with others about policy issues. Historically, only a small percentage of the public is even this active. Even so, the percentage could rise as technology makes public involvement easier and as policy makers become more interested in having a higher level of public participation in government. Most government agencies already make a concerted effort to promote the use of their web sites, to offer information and public services through e-government, and to invite the public to engage the issues. Many of Korea's e-government initiatives have won international acclaim and are benchmarked by other nations looking for examples to copy.

Nearly universal access to the Internet should make it easier for citizens to become active in public affairs. However, like public policy students, every citizen must also be alert to bias in Internet-based information. Each person must learn to ask about the source of the data and how reliable it is. Despite the difficulties, there are reasons to be optimistic about the potential of the Internet and citizen access to information about government and public policy.

Policy analysts have long recognized different social goals furthered by public involvement in policy making and the criteria by which participation can be evaluated. Beierle and Cayford (2002) identify five goals: (1) incorporating public values into decisions; (2) improving the substantive quality of those decisions (for example, by suggesting alternatives and findings errors of incorporate assumptions underlying policy proposals); (3) resolving conflict among the various competing interests (by emphasizing collaborative rather than adversarial decision making); (4) building trust in institutions and processes (thereby improving their ability to solve public problems); (5) educating and informing the public (raising public understanding of the issues and building a shared perspective on possible solutions).

[Figure 12-3] Public Involvement Can Build Trust in Institutions Like the National Assembly

Government agencies and public officials are often unclear about what they expect public participation to accomplish, and citizens might be puzzled as well. Some agencies feign interest in public involvement to appear to be doing the "right thing" and to comply with legal mandates while greatly limiting the degree to which citizens can affect decision making. Responding to that common practice, some analysts have suggested that there are four quite different models of citizen involvement, with increasing degrees of public influence on decision making. The first is the commentary model, in which agencies and proponents dominate. Second is the social learning model, in which citizens learn about policy proposals and provide advice on them. Third is the joint planning model, in which citizens engage in a dialogue with policy makers and planners and work collaboratively with them. Fourth is the consent and consensus model, in which citizens share authority with government and work together to solve problems.

Discussion Questions:

1. How can policy analysts impact government?
2. How can you explain the discrepancy between popular and evidence-based assessments of government?
3. What can the policy process do for citizen participation?

Vocabulary

policy capacity	*public participation*
commentary model	*joint planning model*
social learning model	*consent and consensus model*

References

Beierle, Thomas C. and Cayford, Jerry 2002. *Democracy in Practice: Public Participation in Environmental Decisions.* Washington, D.C.: Resources for the Future.

Bok, Derek. 2001. *The Trouble with Government.* Cambridge: Harvard University Press.

Kraft, Michael E. and Furlong, Scott R. 2004. *Public Policy: Politics, Analysis, and Alternatives.* Washington, D.C.: CQ Press.

Mackenzie, G. Calvin, and Labiner, Judith M. 2002. "Opportunity Lost: The Rise and Fall of Trust and Confidence in Government after September 11." Washington, D.C.: Brookings Institution, Center for Public Service. Available at www.brook.edu.

Putnam, Robert D. 1995. "Tuning In, Tuning Out: The Strange Disappearance of Social Capital in America." *PS: Political Science and Politics, 28* (December): 664-683.

Schneider, Anne L. and Ingram, Helen 1997. *Policy Design for Democracy.* Lawrence, Kansas: University Press of Kansas.

Week 13 & 14 Student Presentation

These weeks are reserved for student projects. Students must do a group project in English. The projects are designed as group projects in order to prepare students for the collaborative nature of policy work.

Group Size

Each project must be prepared and presented in a group of three students. If there are unusual considerations due to the size of the class, the professor may adjust the group size. However, no work should go forward until the group has received the approval of the professor.

Project Length

The project must be presented to the class in English. The presentation should last less than ten minutes, with an additional ten minutes allotted for discussion time.

Paper Submission

A written version of the entire project must be submitted to the professor after revisions. The written version should match the contents of the oral presentation and should be less than 20 pages in length.

Topics

Groups can choose any single public policy for the research topic. The group should agree on the topic and get the professor's approval before they begin research. Policies may be chosen from any general policy area. Policy areas that may be addressed include the economy, industrial policy, defense, energy, trade, cultural policy, social welfare, the environment, education, healthcare, foreign policy, tourism, transportation, construction, law enforcement, and any other policy area approved by the professor.

Contents

The presentation and paper should include the following contents:

- What the issue is
- How the issue entered the public agenda
- What the goal is
- How the goal is achieved
- Who the actors are
- Who wins and loses

Presenting in English

Remember the audience. No speech can be one-size-fits-all. Make sure to set clear objectives at the start to orient the audience and prepare them for what to expect. Try to respond to the audience's expectations and tailor your content to the audience by presenting the information they need to know. Finally, make the presentation interesting and get the audience involved.

Organize your information. Make a clear structure that you readily understand and can remember. Design your introduction and conclusion for the greatest impact. Practice delivering your message within the allowed time. Share your structure to help forge links with the audience.

Use visuals effectively. Design them to present information that highlights aspects of your presentation for maximum impact. Practice handling visuals to use them smoothly. Choose a clear and simple presentation format to highlight important information. Give handouts if necessary.

Use body language. Be relaxed, positive, and confident to help relax the audience and set them at ease. Use eye contact to engage the audience. Use limited body movement to focus attention and highlight meaning, but avoid distracting mannerisms that take away from your message.

Deliver your message effectively. Pace yourself carefully. Adjust your language to fit the audience. Be prepared to slow down and use easier vocabulary to present to an audience with more limited comprehension. Remember that your audience is made up of students like you, so prepare a presentation that you would want to listen to.

Prepare thoroughly. Practice and refer to brief notes during the presentation. Do not plan to read your presentation.

Introduction

Introduce the title and subject of your presentation or your section of the presentation. Highlight the main points of your talk. Acknowledge the audience, and try to form a human bond with them by identifying with their situation (I know you have to listen to a lot of talks today, so I will try to keep this brief). Then transition to the actual message of the speech.

The Body

The body should include all of the contents required for the presentation. Each student should present his or her part in turn. Students should use parallel language in a parallel structure to refer to the topics and points of the presentation. Repetition of key concepts is okay as the audience has no written work in front of them for reference.

Be careful not to repeat the same information mindlessly over and over.

The Conclusion

The closing repeats and reviews the main points of the presentation, as well as the supporting arguments of the body.

Transitions between Students

Practice the speech beforehand to make sure that it fits the allotted time. Make sure that each student knows where to be at every time and that the next student is ready to go when the current speaker is finished.

If you are using Powerpoint or some other visuals, the student who is using the visual should not be the next speaker. With three students, one should be speaking, one should be ready to speak, and one should be handling the visuals.

Rules

Finally, here are some basic rules of presentation.

Be Clear

You have done a lot of research and know a lot about your topic. The audience does not. Make your subject as clear as possible. Define terms, and repeat where possible.

Be Organized

Have an outline and a plan. Practice the presentation in advance. Know what you will do when something goes wrong. Be ready to ask for help and know what sort of help you will need.

Keep track of time. Prepare less than you think you will need to fill the time, but be ready for it to go over time and have a plan for how to cut things down to time. In addition, make sure that you have materials to add detail if your presentation ends up being too short.

Be Interesting

Remember your audience. The best way to keep their attention is by doing things to pull them in. An unusual approach, visuals, activities, questions to the audience, and an attempt to be entertaining may all help to engage the audience.

Be Positive

A positive and optimistic attitude is a huge determiner of success. You are more likely to succeed if you believe in yourself. Your audience will be more likely to respond in kind if you are positive by encouraging you with positive feedback.

Negativity teaches you that you will not succeed and pulls you back. Why choose to fail when it is hard enough to succeed?

Do Not Read

Reading is about the easiest way to kill a good presentation. Reading discourages clarity (unless you are trained to read for an audience). Reading is harder to organize as you cannot add or drop material very easily. You cannot pay attention to the audience and their needs while reading. You cannot pay attention to the time while reading. Reading is not very interesting for the listener. It is difficult to project a positive attitude while you are reading. Reading is often an indication that you have a negative attitude and do not trust yourself.

Do Not Go for Too Long

No one ever complains that a speech is too short. When you go a minute over the audience will start to dislike a good speech. One of the easiest things you can do to gain audience appreciation is by keeping good time. Going on for too long is extremely selfish and inconsiderate of the needs of others.

Bibliography

Affholter, Dennis P. 1994. "Outcome Monitoring." In *Handbook of Practical Program Evaluation.* Ed. Joseph S. Wholey, Harry P. Harty, and Kathryn E. Newcomer. San Francisco: Josse Bass.

"Aging Society Starts in the Provinces." *English Chosun*, April 26, 2005, from http://english.chosun.com/w21data/html/news/200504/200504260021.html

Allision, Graham. 1971. *Essence of Decision: Explaining the Cuban Missile Crisis.* Boston: Little, Brown.

Anderson, James E. 2000. *Public Policy Making.* 4th ed. Boston: Houghton Mifflin.

Anderson, James E. 2003. *Public Policy Making.* 5th ed. Boston: Houghton Mifflin.

Bardach, Eugene. 2000. *A Practical Guide for Policy Analysis: The Eightfold Path to More Effective Problem Solving.* New York: Chatham House.

Baumgartner, Frank R. and Jones, Bryan D. 1993. *Agendas and Instability in American Politics.* Chicago: University of Chicago Press.

Beierle, Thomas C. and Cayford, Jerry 2002. *Democracy in Practice: Public Participation in Environmental Decisions.* Washington, D.C.: Resources for the Future.

Bendor, Jonathan and Hammond, Thomas H. 1992. "Rethinking Allison's Models." *American Political Science Review*, 86 (2).

Bennet, Colin J. and Howlett, Michael. 1992. "The Lessons of Learning: Reconciling Theories of Policy Learning and Policy Change." *Policy Sciences*, 25 (3): 275-294.

Berry, Jeffery M. 1989. "Subgovernments, Issue Networks, and Political Conflict." *Remaking American Politics*. Ed. Richard Sidney and Milkis Harris. Boulder, Colorado: Westview Press.

Bickers, Kenneth N. and Williams, John T. 2001. *Public Policy Analysis: A Political Economy Approach.* Boston, Massachusetts: Houghton-Mifflin.

Birkland, Thomas A. 2001. *An Introduction to the Policy Process: Theories, Concepts, and Models of Public Policy Making.* New York: M. E. Sharpe.

Bok, Derek. 2001. *The Trouble with Government.* Cambridge: Harvard University Press.

"Boss of South Korea Retail Giant Lotte Apologises for Family Feud, Vows Reform." 2015. *The Straights Times*, August 11, 2015 from http://www.straitstimes.com/asia/east-asia/boss-of-south-korea-retail-giant-lotte-apologises-for-family-feud-vows-reform

Cho, Chung-un. 2014. "Sewol Disaster Reveals Failure of Mass Media as Watchdog." *Korea Herald*, May 16, 2014 from http://www.koreaherald.com/view.php?ud=20140516001217

Choe, Sanghyun. 2015. "Adultery is No Longer an Affair of the State in South Korea," February 26, 2015 from http://www.nytimes.com/2015/02/27/world/asia/south-korea-strikes-down-adultery-law.html

Cigler, Allan J. 1991. "Interest Groups: A Subfield in Search of an Identity." *Political Science, Looking to the Future: Volume IV: American Institutions*, ed. Evanston, Illinois: Northwestern University Press.

Cochran, Clarke E., Mayer, Lawrence C., Carr, T. R., Cayer, N. Joseph, McKenzie, Mark J., and Peck, Laura R. 1999. *American Public Policy: An Introduction.* 6th ed. New York: St. Martin's Press.

Cohen, Michael D., March, James G. and Olson, Johan P. 1972. "A Garbage Can Model of Organization Choice." *Administrative Science Quarterly*, 17:1-25.

"Constitution of the Republic of Korea" from http://korea.na.go.kr/res/low_01_read.jsp

"Consumer Groups Urge Lotte Boycott." 2015. *English Chosun*, August 5, 2015 from http://english.chosun.com/site/data/html_dir/2015/08/05/2015080501247.html

Derthick, Martha. 1972. *New Towns in Town.* Washington, DC: Urban Institute.

Dery, David. 1984. *Problem Definition in Policy Analysis.* Lawrence, Kansas: University Press of Kansas.

Dunn, N. William. 1981. *An Introduction to Public Policy Analysis.* Englewood Cliffs, New Jersey: Prentice-Hall, Inc.

Dye, Thomas R. 1992. *Understanding Public Policy.* 7th ed. Englewood Cliffs, New Jersey: Prentice-Hall, Inc.

Dye, R. Thomas. 1995. *Understanding Public Policy.* 8th ed. Englewood Cliffs, New Jersey: Prentice-Hall, Inc.

Easton, David. 1965. *A Systems Analysis of Political Life.* New York: John Wiley.

Elazar, Daniel J. 1984. *American Federalism: A view from the States.* 3rd ed. New York: Harper and Row.

Fischer, Frank, Miller, Gerald J., and Sidney, Mara S. (eds.). 2007. *Handbook of Public Policy Analysis: Theory, Politics, and Methods.* Boca Raton, Florida: CRC Press.

Frohock, Fred M. 1979. *Public Policy: Scope and Logic.* Englewood Cliffs, New Jersey: Prentice Hall.

Gerston, Larry N. 2010. *Public Policy Making: Process and Principles.* Armonk, New York: M.E. Sharpe.

Goggin, Malcolm L., Bowman, Anne O'M., Lester, James P., and O'Toole, Laurence, J. 1990. *Implementation Theory and Practice: Toward a Third Generation.* Glenview, Illinois: Scott Foresman/Little Brown.

Goldenberg, Jacob, David Mazursky, and Sorin Solomon. 1999. "Creative Sparks." *Science*, 3 (September): 1495-1496.

Gupta, Dipak K. 2001. *Analyzing Public Policy: Concepts, Tools, and Techniques.* Washington, DC: Congressional Quarterly.

Ingram, Helen, and Mann, Dean. 1980. "Policy Failure: An Issues Deserving Attention." In *Why Policies Succeed or Fail.* Ingram, Helen, and Mann, Dean. Ed. Beverly Hils, California: Sage.

Jansson, Bruce K. 2003. *Becoming an Effective Policy Advocate.* Pacific Grove, California: Brooks/Cole.

Kang, Jin-Kyu. 2015. "3-Day Weekend for Liberation Day." *Korea JoongAng Daily.* August 5, 2015, from http://koreajoongangdaily.joins.com/news/article/Article.aspx?aid=3007504

Katz, Daniel and Kahn, Robert L. 1966. "Organizations and the System Concept." pp. 206-216, in Shafritz, Jay, Hyde, Alan and Parkes, Sandra (eds). 2004 *Classics of Public Administration,* 5th ed. Belmont, California: Wadsworth.

Kim, Heejin. 2015. "Jobless Rate for Young Koreans Rises to 11.1%." *Korea JoongAng Daily.* March 19, 2015 from http://koreajoongangdaily.joins.com/news/article/Article.aspx?aid=3002087

Kingdon, John W. 1995. *Agendas, Alternatives and Public Policies.* 2nd ed. New York: Harper Collins.

Kraft, Michael E. and Furlong, Scott R. 2004. *Public Policy: Politics, Analysis, and Alternatives.* Washington, D.C.: CQ Press.

Laumann, Edward O. and Knoke, David. 1987. *The Organizational State: Social Choice in National Policy Domains.* Madison: University of Wisconsin Press.

Lee, Jong Youl and Anderson, Chad. 2008. *Policy Analysis.* Seoul: Daeyoung Moonhwasa.

Levi, Edward. 1949. *An Introduction to Legal Reasoning.* Chicago: University of Chicago Press.

Levine, Charles H., Peters, B. Guy, and Thompson, Frank J. 1990. *Public Administration: Challenges, Choices, Consequences.* Glenview, Illinois: Scott, Foresman/Little Brown.

Lindblom, Charles E. 1959. "The Science of Muddling Through." *Public Administration Review,* 19: 79-88.

Lowi, Theodore J. 1964. "American Business, Public Policy, Case Studies, and Political Theory." *World Politics,* 16 (July): 667-715.

Lowi, Theodore. 1979. *The End of Liberalism: The Second Republic of the United States.* 2nd ed. New York: W.W. Norton.

Mackenzie, G. Calvin, and Labiner, Judith M. 2002. "Opportunity

Lost: The Rise and Fall of Trust and Confidence in Government after September 11." Washington, D.C.: Brookings Institution, Center for Public Service. Available at www.brook.edu.

MacRae, Duncan and Wilde, James. 1979. *Policy Analysis for Public Decisions.* North Scituate, Massachusetts: Duxbury.

Majone, Giandomenico. 1989. *Evidence, Argument, and Persuasion in the Policy Process.* New Haven: Yale University Press.

May, Peter. 1990. "Reconsidering Policy Design: Policies and Publics." *Journal of Public Policy,* 11 (2): 187-206.

Mazmanian, Daniel A. and Kraft, Michael E. eds. 1999. *Toward Sustainable Communities: Transition and Transformations in Environmental Policy.* Cambridge: MIT Press.

Ministry of Employment and Labor. 2015. "Major Statistics," August 10, 2015, from http://www.moel.go.kr/english/pas/pasMajor.jsp

Nagel, Stuart S. 2002. *Handboook of Public Policy Evaluation.* Thousand Oaks, California: Sage.

Nakamura, Robert T. 1987. "The Textbook Policy Process and Implementation Research." *Policy Studies Journal,* 7(1): 142-154.

Neustadt, Richard E. 1990. *Presidential Power and the Modern Presidents: The Politics of Leadership from Roosevelt to Reagan.* New York: Free Press.

Olson, Mancur. 1971. *The Logic of Collective Action.* Cambridge: Harvard University Press.

Parsons, Wayne. 1995. *Public Policy: An Introduction to the Theory and Practice of Policy Analysis.* Northampton, Massachusetts: Edward Elgar.

Patton, Carl V. and Sawicki, David S. 1993. *Basic Methods of Policy Analysis and Planning.* 2nd ed. Englewood Cliffs, New Jersey: Prentice Hall, Inc.

Percy-Smith, Janie. 1996. *Needs Assessments in Public Policy.* Bristol, Pennsylvania: Open University Press.

Peters, B. Guy. 1999. *American Public Policy: Promise and Performance.* Chappaqua, New York: Chatham House/Seven Rivers.

"Powers of the National Assembly" from http://korea.na.go.kr/

int/aut_01.jsp?leftid=CA

Pressman, Jeffrey and Wildavsky, Aaron. 1973. *Implementation.* Berkeley, California: University of California Press.

Putnam, Robert D. 1995. "Tuning In, Tuning Out: The Strange Disappearance of Social Capital in America." *PS: Political Science and Politics*, 28 (December): 664-683.

Randall R. Bovbjerg. 1985. "What Is Policy Analysis?." *Journal of Policy Analysis and Management*, 5(1), Autumn: 154-158.

Ringquist, Evan J. 1993. *Environmental Protection at the State Level: Politics and Progress in Controlling Pollution.* Armonk, New York: M. E. Sharpe.

Ripley, Randall and Franklin, Grace. 1991. *Congress, the Bureaucracy and Public Policy.* 5th ed. Pacific Grove, California: Brooks-Cole.

Ryan, Neal. 1995. "Unraveling Conceptual Developments in Implementation Analysis". *Australian Journal of Public Administration*, 54 (1): 65-81.

Sabatier, Paul A. 1988. "An Advocacy Coalition Framework of Policy Change and the Role of Policy-Oriented Learning Therein." *Policy Sciences*, 21: 129-168.

Sabatier, Paul A. 1991. "Political Science and Public Policy." *PS: Political Science and Politics*, 24 (2): 144-147.

Sabatier, Paul A. 2007. "The Need for Better Theories," pp. 3-17 in Sabatier, Paul A. (ed), *Theories of the Policy Process,* 2nd ed. Boulder, Colorado: Westview Press.

Schneider, Anne L. and Ingram, Helen. 1997. *Policy Design for Democracy.* Lawrence, Kansas: University Press of Kansas.

Schneider, Anne and Ingram, Helen. 1993. "The Social Construction of Target Populations: Implications for Politics and Policy." *American Political Science Review*, 87 (2): 334-348.

"Seoul City to Lay Off 1,300 Officials." *English Chosun,* November 2, 2007, from http://english.chosun.com/w21data/html/news/200711/200711020018.html

Shin, Yong-Ho, Jeong, Yong-Soo, and Ser, Myo-Ja. 2015 "Gov't

Concludes THAAD is Best Option for Korea." *Korea JoongAng Daily*, May 21, 2015 from http://koreajoongangdaily.joins.com/news/article/Article.aspx?aid=3004458

Simon, Christopher A. 2009. *Public Policy: Preferences and Outcomes*, 2nd ed. New York, New York: Routledge.

Starling, Grover. 1988. *Strategies for Policy Making*. Chicago: Dorsey Press.

Steinberger, Peter J. 1980. "Typologies of Public Policy: Meaning Construction and the Policy Process." *Social Science Quarterly*, 61 (September): 185-197.

Stillman, Richard J. 1996. *The American Bureaucracy*. Chicago: Nelson-Hall.

Stone, Deborah. 1997. *Policy Paradox: The Art of Political Decision Making*. New York: W.W. Norton & Company.

Stokey, Edith and Zeckhauser, Richard. 1978. *A Primer for Policy Analysis*. New York: W.W. Norton & Company.

Theodoulou, Stella Z. and Cahn, Matthew A. 1995. *Public Policy: The Essential Readings*. Upper Saddle River, New Jersey: Prentice-Hall, Inc.

Vedung, Evert. 2005. *Public Policy and Evaluation Program*. New Brunswick, New Jersey: Transaction Publishers.

Weimer, L. David and Vining, R. Aidan. 2005. *Policy Analysis: Concepts and Practice*. Pearson, New Jersey: Prentice-Hall, Inc.

Wildavsky, Aaron. 1964. *The Politics of Budgetary Process*. Boston: Little, Brown.

Wilson, Edward O. 1998. *Consilience: The Unity of Knowledge*. New York: Knopf.

Wilson, Woodrow. 1887. "The Study of Administration." pp. 22-37, in Shafritz, Jay, Hyde, Alan, and Parkes, Sandra (eds). 2004 *Classics of Public Administration*, 5th ed. Belmont, California: Wadsworth.

Wood, B. Dan. 1991. "Federalism and Policy Responsiveness: The Clean Air Case." *Journal of Politics*, 53 (3): 851-859.

"Youth Unemployment in Korea on the Rise." *English Chosun*, December 24, 2007, from http://english.chosun.com/w21data/

html/news/200712/200712240012.html

Zahariadis, Nikolaos. 1993. "To Sell or Not to Sell? Telecommunications Policy in Britain and France." *Journal of Public Policy*, 12(4): 355-376.

Index

Q

R

S

T